The Cheviot
the Stag an[d]
the Black, B[lack Oil]

Probably the best example of truly popular theatre in the seventies, *The Cheviot, the Stag and the Black, Black Oil* tells the continuing story of the exploitation of the Scottish Highlands, first through the Clearances to make way for the cheviot sheep, then by the stag-hunting landed gentry and lately in the name of North Sea Oil. Performed to unparalleled acclaim throughout Scotland by the 7:84 Theatre Company and subsequently televised, the play is printed here in a definitive edition with production photographs and a commentary on the background to the show by the author/director, John McGrath.

Published plays by the same author

EVENTS WHILE GUARDING THE BOFORS GUN
BAKKE'S NIGHT OF FAME
RANDOM HAPPENINGS IN THE HEBRIDES
FISH IN THE SEA
THE GAME'S A BOGEY
LITTLE RED HEN
YOBBO NOWT
JOE'S DRUM
BLOOD RED ROSES & SWINGS AND ROUNDABOUTS

Also by John McGrath

A GOOD NIGHT OUT
— Popular Theatre: Audience, Class and Form

John McGrath

THE CHEVIOT,
THE STAG AND
THE BLACK, BLACK OIL

presented by

EYRE METHUEN · LONDON

First published in this revised, illustrated edition in 1981
by Eyre Methuen Ltd, 11 New Fetter Lane, London EC4P 4EE
Originally published in 1974 by West Highland Publishing Co,
Breakish, Isle of Skye IV42 8PY
Copyright © 1974, 1981 by John McGrath
ISBN 0 413 48880 2

CAUTION
All rights in this play are strictly reserved and application for
performance etc should be made before rehearsal *either* to 7:84
Theatre Company, 58 Queen Street, Edinburgh EH2 3NS *or* to
Margaret Ramsay Ltd, 14a Goodwin's Court, St Martin's Lane,
London WC2N 4LL. No performance may be given unless
permission has been obtained.

All photos are by Barry Jones unless stated otherwise.

Printed and bound on Great Britain by Whitstable Litho Ltd.,
Whitstable, Kent
Set in IBM 10pt Journal by 🅰 Tek-Art, Croydon, Surrey

The Year of the Cheviot

by John McGrath

Our first gig was on Saturday, 31 March, 1973. Bob Tait, then of Scottish International magazine, had got together, in Edinburgh, a conference of 450 people from all over Scotland to discuss what kind of Scotland they wanted. They were politicians, union men, writers, social and community workers, academics, and ordinary people who cared about the future of Scotland. We were to perform our new play for them, before setting off on a six-week tour of the Highlands and Islands. The problem was, as I explained to Bob, by the 16th March we'd only just got the company together, and not a line of the play was written. Could he find somebody else? No. That was what he wanted.

Well, we were scheduled to finish most of the writing by the 31st, so we said would he accept a reading? It was a public play, about Scottish history, and there would be people there who were expert in all kinds of areas. Why couldn't we present it as a work in progress, and throw it open to discussion? We could learn a lot, and use intelligent criticism constructively. We had another two weeks to rehearse and finalise the show. Why not let the public in on the process — we could only benefit, and they might even enjoy it? Bob agreed.

On Friday night I stayed up until four writing the last scene. On Saturday we read it, discussed it, rehearsed the songs, changed a few, then went over, with twitching bottles, to face 450 people.

It was the best thing we could have done. The audience at the end rose to its feet and cheered, then poured out advice, corrections, support, suggestions of great practical value, facts, figures, books, sources, and above all enthusiasm. Not because we'd been 'good' or 'clever' — but because what we were struggling to say was what they, and masses of people in Scotland, wanted said. Now.

One hundred shows, over 30,000 people, and 17,000 miles later, we feel even more strongly that the strength of the show is in the expression of what people all over Scotland want to say. Many have come for the entertainment — there are good laughs, good acting, good singing, good fiddling — but nearly all go away heightened in their awareness of what has been, and is being done to the people of the Highlands, in the savage progress of capitalism. And they want to hear it.

*   *   *

I'd spent quite a lot of time in the Highlands before anyone mentioned the Clearances. And then it was only indirectly. In 1961, someone I'd got to know came round for a drink, and said he'd discovered some old parish registers. This valley used to support 253 families, he said. Now you'd be lucky to find 50.

Then came the stories. From all corners. How the Gaelic language had been suppressed. How the Dukes of Sutherland were hated for what they did when they discovered there was more profit in sheep than in people — how their factors burnt the houses, drove the people to the sea-coast, herded them into boats for Canada, all to make way for the Cheviot sheep, how they forced every tenant to pay one shilling towards the huge statue of the Duke on top of Ben Bhraggie — and at the same time the Sutherlands were building Dunrobin Castle to vie with Versailles in opulence and conspicuous consumption — not to mention running Stafford House in London, where the Sutherlands spent most of their time, living in a style surpassing that of the richest in Europe.

Later, John Prebble's book *The Highland Clearances* did an excellent job in bringing this neglected episode of nineteenth century history to a wider public, as did Ian Grimble's very thorough account in *The Trial of Patrick Sellar*. To me, at that time, it was a source of amazement that so little was known of it outside, even inside, Scotland. To the people there, it was, and is, a burning memory, never to be forgotten, and never forgiven. As late as 1970, the Sutherlands' factor was greeted with Baas, and cries of 'Men not Sheep' when he got up rashly to ask a question at a Labour election meeting in Golspie.

For years the Highlands have, to most people, been shrouded in mist. Either the mist of romanticism — the land of solitary splendour, Gaelic twilight, and sturdy, independent, gently-spoken crofters. Or the mists of inevitable backwardness — a land that missed the boat, with no resources and a dwindling population, a land inhabited by lazy, shifty, dreamers who cannot be helped, in which nothing can alter.

The realities of Highland life, and of the Highland people, are very different. The realities are created by the actions of a feudal system leaping red in tooth and claw into an imperialist capitalist system, becoming more repressive, more violent as it does so.

Another reality is that it *can*, and *must* be changed.

*   *   *

At the first sniff of oil off the east coast of Scotland, things began to jump. First in Aberdeen and the North-East. Then all over. Suddenly villages that did not merit even an advance factory for 100 workers are being taken over by thousands of men in labour camps building oil-rigs, and oil-production platforms. The Highlands and Islands Development Board had failed to do anything about Stornoway's 150 unemployed. Now Fred Olsen's men are talking about Stornoway's need for 5,000 jobs: it happens they want to service and build rigs there. They're even talking about a shipyard. Land prices in some areas have been so inflated by speculators that local farmers can't stay, and in Aberdeen young couples in need of houses are talking about emigrating. International corporations — oil, land, property, building, construction, marine, even catering — are jumping about all over the place looking for millions of dollars. And they don't care what they do to the people to get them. Capitalism has seen another big opportunity in the Highlands.

*   *   *

It was with this perspective in mind that three of us who had been working with 7:84 Theatre Company decided to go to Scotland, try to form a Scottish 7:84, and take a play about the Highlands 'from the time of the Clearances up to the present day', around village halls, dance halls, community centres and schools in the North. David MacLennan had, amongst many other things, worked on administration, stage management, lighting, driving, and general political determination since 7:84's first play *Trees in the Wind*, in 1971. Elizabeth MacLennan also had been a founder of the company, had acted with it since *Trees in the Wind*, and taken part in all its activities. Both knew the

Highlands intimately, and cared about them passionately — from personal involvement, and as part of their overall socialist commitment.

The English 7:84 went into rehearsal for a tour of Adrian Mitchell's *Man Friday*. We went to Scotland and began to look for people who cared enough for the idea to come and work harder, mentally and physically, than most reckon possible, for not much more than the Equity minimum. We thought of advertising, but the demands looked too ridiculous: Needed: people who can act, sing, entertain, and play at least one musical instrument (all superbly well), who are committed socialists, know the Highlands, can drive, and are prepared to join in all the work of the company on a communal basis, and play in a dance-band. Apply 7:84 (Scotland).

Amazingly enough, we didn't run the ad. But the people came. Three actors I had seen in *The Welly Boot Show* the year before, Alex Norton, Bill Paterson and John Bett. They had worked together a great deal before, and combined an enormous number of skills, acting, singing, guitar, pipes, whisky, commitment, and others. Yet another MacLennan — Dolina, from Lewis in the Outer Hebrides, no relation to the other two. She spoke only Gaelic until she was eight, sang Gaelic songs the way they should be sung, and had years of experience of holding an audience. Chris Martin, who had just walked out of a steady job with a publishing company, and had worked in Chile, South Africa and India, came, in the first instance, to work on publicity. And Allan Ross, fiddler extraordinary, musician, entertainer, whose great-great grandfather had been cleared from Easter Ross. Ferelith Lean came with us to freeze on countless makeshift box-offices, and dish out the wages. That was the new company. When we met to discuss the way the collective should work, it felt very good.

*   *   *

Obviously I, as a writer, had a very clear idea of exactly how I wanted the show to be. I knew who it was for, and I knew what I wanted to say and how I wanted to say it. But I also wanted everybody in the company to be intimately involved in the actual process of creating it. I had always fought shy of group-writing before, and still do. This wasn't to be a free-for-all, utopian fantasy: I wouldn't expect to play Allan Ross's fiddle,

*Allan Ross, fiddler
extraordinary*

or to sing in Gaelic, or act. The company didn't expect to write
the play. My contribution was my experience as a writer and
director, and it was to be used. But there were two things we
could do to break down the insane hierarchies of the theatre.
Firstly, we could all respect each other's skills and at the same
time lay them open for collective discussion and advice. Secondly,
we could work as equal human beings, no skill being elevated
over another, no personal power or superiority being assumed
because of the nature of the individual contribution: no stars, of
any kind. And no recourse to the 'I'm an artist' pose to
camouflage either power-seeking or avoidance of responsibility
to the collective.

So we all sat down, with blank note-pads. I outlined the
sixteen main areas or blocks of the play, and how I thought we
should approach each one. There was a huge pile of books,
cuttings Elizabeth had kept, and other material on the next table.
Everyone was given one or two areas to be personally responsible
for, check what we said, and answer to in public discussion. For
example, Bill was given the section on the Highland's military
tradition — the numbers killed in the wars, the way recruiting
worked, etc, and he looked through the books, went to libraries,
and military museums to get the facts. When we came to write
that section, I knew what I wanted to write, we all discussed it,
Bill knew the details, or where he could find them, and either

there, with everybody present, or in the evening at home, the
section was written.

The form of the play was conducive to this kind of approach.
One truly popular form of entertainment in the Highlands,
past and present is the ceilidh. This is usually a gathering at
which all, or most, of those present, with or without the aid of
the whisky, sing a song, tell a story, play an instrument, have a
good blether, and occasionally end up dancing until the next
morning. In the past, these gatherings had also had their political
side, particularly at the time of the Land Leagues, and stories of
Highland history and oppression had been passed on. In the West,
they were also one way of keeping intact the Gaelic Culture —
language, literature, songs and manners. 'Ceilidh parties' also go
from place to place to entertain and be entertained, and are very
popular. I wanted to keep this form — an assembly of songs,
stories, scenes, talk, music and general entertainment — and to
tell through it the story of what had happened and is now
happening to the people. And to end the evening with a dance,
for people to get a chance to talk and have a good time. But
more of that later.

As we worked, our knowledge of the subject grew. We invited
sympathetic friends with special knowledge in certain areas to
come and talk to us. Ray Burnett, for example, who had been
beavering away on the history of the Land Leagues. The day he
came to talk to us, he had uncovered evidence of soldiers back
from the 1914-18 war occupying land in Sutherland — a phenome-
non not mentioned in the history books. After the session, I
wrote a song about it. When we performed in Sutherland, the
song aroused memories — and old men who had been on those
land-raids, and many who just knew them, came up to us with
stories that would make a decent chapter in a decent history of
Scotland, if there were such a thing. And would certainly give
the lie to the convenient myth that the Highlanders took it all
with a tug of the forelock.

Ray, and our own sources, provided us with a problem. We
wanted to tell what happened on Skye in the 1880s, particularly
in the Braes area, where the resistance to the landlord was
particularly effective. The problem was, we had too much
material — enough for six scenes, let alone one. After two days,
during which the story had been hammered out into a strong
narrative, we were desperate. How could we tell so much in a
short time? I crept off into a corner of the disused discotheque

we were working in, and wrote a ballad. Somebody saw a verse, came up with a tune. We all threw in ideas for the chorus. Some verses got thrown out, others improved. We moved on.

After two weeks huddling round a table, occasionally leaping over to the musical instruments to try something, or moving into the open space to see how a scene might move, we had something to begin to work with. Not the purist's improvised theatre. Not 'collective creativity', or group therapy. But a written text that all the company were part of, and deeply involved in, and excited about. Nobody had anything to do that they thought was wrong, everybody knew exactly why every word was there.

And the company had grown in knowledge, concern for the subject and conviction, through the process. So we went off to Bob Tait's reading.

With the boost of that audience's reaction, and the excitement about the subject we already had, rehearsals became fast and enjoyable. I had no desire to play the conventional director, to pull strings secretly and have heart-to-hearts about problems. I threw the material at the company, told them they were entertainers now, not Chekovian actors, and to work on their acts, and bring them in for us all to see. Being good Scottish actors — who had all worked in many different situations, from Ibsen via panto to spieling on strip-shows, that is what they did. I, and the others, threw in ideas, made sure one part related well to all the other parts, that the political meaning didn't get lost in the gagging or the singing — in fact, that they *were* part of the political meaning — and generally stood back from it all a bit, to provide the necessary objective perspective. After the next two weeks, we began to need an audience again.

All this time, as well as writing and rehearsing, the company was simultaneously trying to turn itself into a dance band, with at least four hours of dance music at the ready. The dance after the show as I have said, was an essential part of the evening. The task we set ourselves — to provide the music — was formidable. Allan was a brilliant fiddler, with a vast knowledge of Highland fiddle music. Elizabeth, a pianist, had prepared herself by mastering the accordion in six weeks flat. Alex had amazing facility on the guitar, and played rhythm along with the bass line. Bill and Doli sang, Bill played whistles, pipes, piano and I'm not sure what else besides. There the musical talent ended. I fancied myself on the drums, Dave thought he

'Elizabeth mastered the accordion in six weeks flat . . .'

' . . . Alex had amazing facility on the guitar'

might come to terms with the bass guitar. We both got fired by the others after a week, for enthusiastic incompetence. We managed without a bass, and asked Tommy Marshall, an Edinburgh drummer, to join us for the dances, which, to our relief, he did. He also drove, sold the programmes at the beginning of the play, and joined in the general work.

Our basic sound was traditional Highland dance music — waltzes, eightsome reels, schottishes, Gay Gordons, etc — and the band providing this was christened the Force Ten Gaels. But we did want to be able to throw in, in some places, a load of rock and more modern sounds, so we created in honour of Alex Norton, the Nortones, with Allan dropping the fiddle and playing electric bass.

Night after night, after a hard day's work, we assembled and rehearsed material, decided on a programme that might work, and slowly began to play with a little confidence and togetherness. It almost began to sound like a band.

* * *

Before rehearsals David and Chris Martin had set off, after long

The Force Ten Gaels

consultations, to the places we were hoping to play. Between us, we had friends or contacts in almost every corner of the North, and they soon made many more friends in the others. The response to what they were proposing was one first of amazement, then of enthusiasm, and then of overwhelming practical kindness. People willingly took on the jobs of sticking up posters, selling tickets, spreading the word, finding accommodation, sometimes even providing it. Dave and Chris booked the halls on the spot, in as sensible an order as they could, balancing free dates, mileage, rival attractions and estimated exhaustion with remarkable dexterity.

The Scottish Arts Council Drama Committee had at first displayed incredulity. They thought Highlanders didn't want to know about the Clearances, the politics of oil and such, and anyway wouldn't pay to see a theatre-show because they didn't go to the theatre. They threw our estimated budget back in our face, and turned down our request for a small guarantee against loss. We went back armed with the response, and the figures Chris and Dave had got, and a lengthy explanation of why we thought it would work as we estimated. They had second thoughts, gave us the small guarantee, and have proved more generous ever since. As it happened, our figures were almost exactly right: the Highlanders *did* want to hear their true history told out loud, and they certainly wanted to say something about the politics of oil. An ancient, near-blind, Gaelic poet, the Bard of Melbost, came up to us after a show in the Outer Hebrides, and said: 'I have heard the story of my people told with truth. If I die tonight, I die a happier man.' He, too, had been paying taxes to support the Arts Council. For the first time, he was getting something back. I hope it won't be the last.

*   *   *

Our first gig was in Aberdeen. We had one van borrowed from the original 7:84, that sort of went. I spent the last of my fee for writing a movie that never got made on another Transit, with seats. We were on the road, north. The word of mouth from the *What Kind of Scotland?* reading was good, several Aberdonians had been there, and it had had good notices in the papers. Even so, we were surprised to hear the Arts Centre was full. The show went well, for a first night, and we were staggered to see an Aberdeen audience stand up and cheer at the end. The last section of the show, on the oil rip-off, had meant so much

The van unloading in the Orkneys (Photo: Robin Worrall)

to them, they demanded that we come back (which we did, with pleasure, a few months later). Fortunately, as this was one of the few places we played with theatre-type fixed seating, we couldn't follow with a dance. In the next few days, now the show was on, the band grabbed every minute to rehearse a lot more, and didn't face the public until the next Saturday night, in Rosemarkie hall, on the Black Isle. We were saved there by the imminent arrival of the Sabbath, which meant we had to finish the dance at 11.45, as is the custom on the Highland Saturday, having provided an hour and a half's pretty convincing music: but that was about all we had. The band rehearsed on, and by the following Tuesday really gave one of the best dances, we, or Kinlochbervie, had experienced for some time.

Kinlochbervie was the beginning of the real Highland tour. Aberdeen, Stirling, Inverness and Rosemarkie in the first week had been exciting enough. The Chairman of the Highlands and Islands Development Board, which comes in for some rough handling in the play, turned up, with a lot of the staff. He had both legs in plaster, and wore a kilt. I anticipated a rallentando of an exit — it was the same man who, as our Ambassador in Indonesia, had marched around the grounds of the besieged embassy playing the bagpipes to the enragement of the already overheated Djakartans — but, whether through inability or masochism, he stayed to the end. It seems to be a deliberate tactic of the ruling class under attack in public, at least in the Highlands, to be seen sportingly taking it on the chin, thereby eliciting admiration from the people they are exploiting for their courage, pluck or open-mindedness.

The Countess of Sutherland did the same trick, many months later in Golspie, and ensured that the 'Aberdeen Press and Journal' carried a report of her sporting gesture. As half of the play is a direct attack on her forebears, and the other half an attack on present-day landowners, which she is, she probably got more than she bargained for, but a few of her tenants were impressed — though not, by any means, all. It is notable, though, how far the ruling classes will go to appear impervious to any articulate opposition. As one tweedy lady on Skye said to her tweedy husband: 'It's so nice to be able to laugh at oneself.' Against which, to discomfort her blandness, I can only quote a twelve-year-old boy from nearby: 'It'll be great round here when all this starts happening — when people start demanding their rights.'

But to Kinlochbervie. It's a few miles down the West Coast from Cape Wrath, a crofting and fishing community, spread out over wild and beautiful hills, with a new harbour, a hotel for the fishing gentry, and a tiny hall on the edge of the water. We arrived about mid-day, made for the bar, and bumped into a few people Dave, Liz and I knew of old. They were politely surprised that we had actually come, and they and some of the crews from the boats had a bit of an alcoholic get-together with the company. Then we went down to the hall to set up. Already people were waving to us as we drove the vans over, and by the evening the word had brought a full house to see what the hell this was all about. The boats had been kept in by gale-warnings, so the crews came too.

In the halls, we used the stages, normally only big enough for a small band, for our 'scenery'. This was a giant pop-up book, like children's pop-up books, only eight feet deep and ten across, made from strengthened cardboard. As you turn each page, a fresh 'set' pops up from in between the pages, in this instance

The pop-up book

all beautifully constructed and painted by John Byrne, a Glasgow artist and, subsequently, playwright. As well as his own work, he sometimes does record-sleeves, and uses colour, shape and cartoon-effect with great imagination, and wit. In front of the stage, on the floor of the hall, we put up our own platform, 18 inches high, and the company sits on either side, on the same level as the audience, throughout, when they aren't actually doing their bits. That way, we kept closer to the audience, and had the same intimacy whatever kind of hall we were in. We carried our own lights, set up on stands, and operated by David from his seat amongst the others, in full view of the audience, on a small portable six-way board. All the music is live, some electric, some acoustic. In the middle of the front of our stage, there is a mike, used or not used according to what we're doing. Generally not necessary for audibility, but useful for variety of effect.

The show begins as the audience is coming in with Allan playing reels on the fiddle, and the audience, if they feel like it, clapping or stamping their feet in time. From that, Bill introduces the show, and gets the audience to sing a song together — with song-sheets held up by the company. From the way that audience in Kinlochbervie, none of whom had ever been in such a thing as a theatre, reacted to the show, we knew that it was impossible to under-estimate a Highland audience. In knowledge, sophistication, politics, history and wit, they were right there, if not way ahead of us. We had never 'written down' to some supposed audience level. It's just as well we hadn't. Direct Marxist analysis of the Clearances (cf *Das Kapital*), long chunks of readings from eye-witness historical accounts, facts and figures about oil companies and the technicalities of exploration, all were not only grasped but waited for, expected. It's quite a Gaelic speaking area, and even those few who didn't speak the language joined in with Dolina as she sang. In the modern section, there are several songs to which we added new verses almost every day either to refer to local events or keep up with the events as they happen. There were no puzzled looks — everybody knew what was happening. That night in Kinlochbervie, 250 miles north of Glasgow, in that so-called backward area, the people taught us what theatre has to be about. And that was the lesson we learnt over and over again, in fifty or sixty halls all over the North, from Stornoway and Lochmaddy in the Outer Hebrides, to Aberdeen in the east, to Orphir in the Orkneys. They didn't stand up or cheer — that was what it should be, and that was just fine.

Everybody, from grandmas to toddlers, stayed for the dance. The chairs and benches were pushed to the side, props and costumes cleared, band gear set up, and for the first time the band showed it could do it. They had to. The fiddle was a great hit. For many years, fiddles had been destroyed, as ungodly, immoral and conducive to lustful practices. When it sang out again, light shone in a lot of old eyes, and nobody had to be asked to dance. After an eightsome reel, exhausting to dance, even more wearing to play, Dolina got up to sing some more songs in Gaelic. As always thereafter, even the rowdiest crowd settled down to listen and join in. About midnight, the boats had to go out, gale-warnings retracted, but the crews wouldn't go until she sang one for them. So she sang a beautiful old Lewis fisherman's song, that defies translation. It all sounds like romantic twaddle, but that only shows how great the gap is that has been driven between the Gael and his cynical masters. Dolina's seven brothers and her father and his father were fishermen: she wasn't singing out a fantasy, nor did they think so. Off they went. Six months later, we went back to Durness, a few miles away, and the memory of that song stopped a punch-up before it could begin.

About two-thirty we stumbled off, No Alcoholic Beverages having been Consumed On These Premises, of course, to caravans borrowed for the night that nearly took off, gale-warning or no gale-warning, to B & Bs, or (Elizabeth and myself) to the hotel. We had this honour (it being the beginning of the tour) because we had our children with us — two boys, one five, one six — and they had to stay somewhere where there was someone to baby-sit. All the B & B ladies were at the do, and we knew the lady who managed the hotel. This theory could have led to some serious class-distinction, and was quickly eroded, but on that night we were glad the boys had four walls, and not a bucking caravan roped to the rock while we were away. It also gave all of us the way into the hotel lounge, where someone produced a whisky bottle with a few dregs in it, which was passed round as we sat and tried to work out what we felt about the night, the show, the dance, and the audience's feelings about both. We knew we had a lot of work to do still, but we all felt we now knew not only *how* to work on the show, but also, for the first time as a lived experience, why.

*   *   *

The next night was a disaster. Partly because we were tired (the caravanners not having slept at all), grumpy, hung over, our memory of the night before shattered by the grim realities of striking the gear from a hall that needed an Alka-Seltzer, loading the vans, driving to Lochinver, setting it all up again, finding the digs, finding some food, getting ready again. (Though we did see an eagle being mobbed by two buzzards, and Lochinver is one of the most scenically beautiful places in the world.) Partly because of a curious fact about the Highlands. It often happens that two places apparently next to each other on the map, apparently geographically identical, are socially more different than Hampstead from Peking. And when we found not only a different kind of response, but a totally different kind of audience, we didn't altogether cope. The show was passable, it was what we had rehearsed, and everybody was working hard, but it felt uncomfortable.

Lochinver suffers from being inundated by what are known as 'white settlers'. The chief of them all, a butcher from Liverpool now known as Lord Vestey, owns over 100,000 acres of Sutherland, including several fine mountains and the whole of Lochinver. He also owns huge tracts of Australia, Argentina, and Brazil, shipping lines, insurance companies, whaling companies, etc. and is into both the docks at Wapping and Midland Cold Storage, the containerisation people, the row over which put three dockers in gaol. In the play, he figures as an excellent reason for crofters in the Highlands showing international solidarity and solidarity with dockers in London, amongst others.

Apart from him, Lochinver has many minor breeds of white settler, English and Scottish, retired, or living off investments, or just failed gentry come to find a few forelocks that might still be tugged at them. Unfortunately for us, these people had appropriated us in advance, because we were 'theatre' and they were cultivated. Most of the local people had taken their cue and stayed away. We did have a friend who was working on the huge road improvement scheme into the town, and he brought a lot of his mates, but they sat at the back, and enjoyed two shows — one our lot doing the play, and the other the white settlers at the front trying to stomach it. But the participation was minimal, and the laughter inhibited. Then to crown it all, for the first hour and a half of the dance, there were forty men and only one girl — and she didn't want to get up, not surprisingly. Just as we decided to pack it in, three girls arrived all done up and demanded that we play until two. It was then 12.30. One girl — who can best be described as strapping — then proceeded to display such powers of leadership, eloquence, guile, force, righteous indignation and revolutionary fervour that we almost announced we were going to start again just for her. But the rest had gone home, and we simply hadn't the energy. I only hope she meets Lord Vestey one bright day, and gives him the same treatment. If we got our roasting for not restarting a dance at half past midnight, what would she give him for all his crimes against the people?

*   *   *

During the next few weeks, we moved from village to village down the west coast, as far as Dornie (which was one of the best nights of the tour, in every way), then over to Skye, from Skye to Harris, then Lewis, then back from Stornoway to Ullapool, across to the east coast, up to the Orkneys, and back via Thurso to Sutherland again. There were not many Lochinvers, I'm glad to say. One on Skye, now badly overrun. A strange one at Alness, now oil-struck. But mostly direct contact, exciting,

Performing in Dornie Hall, 'one of the best nights of the tour in every way'

enjoyable and effective nights. Orkney was bizarre. Small audiences in Stromness and Kirkwall, the two main towns. On our third, and last night, in Orphir, a small village in between, suddenly hundreds. Apparently nobody in Orkney goes to anything until someone else has gone and reported on it. A curious sensation at the box-office, waiting for a whole island full of people who are all waiting for each other.

At Orphir we had a good dance, marked by several odd moments. One was near the beginning. A large crowd were sizing us up for a bit too long, showing a reluctance we hadn't expected. However, Allan had met an Orcadian fiddler, who was sitting in with the band. After a while Liz asked him what they were all waiting for. The Eva Three Step, he said darkly. After a quick consultation, it turned out you did this particular dance to music we had already played, with little result, for the Gay Gordons. So Bill announced the Evoe Three Step. There was a cheer, the floor filled, and we played the same music all over again. From that moment, the dance took off till early next morning.

You can tell a lot about a community from the way they

dance. In Orkney, during the eightsome, couples pass on from group to group automatically all round the floor, so the whole crowd is all in one big, integrated routine. It may lack the enthusiasm or the heuchs of Sutherland, but it works like clockwork.

At one point, I had to give Tommy a rest from the drums — he'd sprained his wrist. He trusted me on the waltzes, having laboriously knocked all ambition to do more than keep strict time out of my Krupa-based fantasies, so I sat in for a waltz, and concentrated like hell. I was appalled, when, after a few minutes, I looked up to see a crowded floor standing stock-still — everyone of them. I hastily looked back to my drumming, wondering if I was really so bad they'd just stopped altogether and were about to stampede me off the platform. I furtively glanced again, and there they were, like statues again, only this time they'd changed positions. Not to be thrown completely, I didn't look up again for quite a time, waiting for the bottles, etc, to rain down on me from an angry mob of frustrated Orcadian waltzers. When I did look up, they were still immobile, but in different places again. I determined to brazen it out, and see what happened. After a few more bars of freeze, I almost dropped my drumsticks when, as one man, they suddenly leapt frenziedly around the floor then, again as one, they all stood block-like again, to all appearances glazed and baked. It turned out that this was another local craze — the Hesitation Waltz. It vaguely resembled the motions of the St Ola, the ferry to Thurso, though I don't know which was based on which.

*   *   *

We developed a kind of rhythm, to keep us going and to prevent a repetition of the exhaustion of the second night. We travelled, when possible, about eleven in the morning, by road or ferry or both; during the journey, Allan or I drove one van, Dave or Chris the other; everybody else was fairly lively, and, as we were driving through some of the most awe-inspiring country in Europe, we all somehow drew a great deal of strength from just looking out of the window. There were stories of places we were going to or through, songs, jokes, and, for the two boys, school. Apart from lessons from Liz, they were treated to the University of Life, from Bill and Alex, with short courses on jokes, sex-education, wild life, songs, stories, poems, more jokes and Scottish history. They kept diaries with drawings of events and

'The University of Life': Elizabeth MacLennan, Alex Norton and and the two boys at Lochinver

places, and brought their own energy and imagination to the whole proceedings. We either stopped on the way or found some food and a drink on arrival, met a few people, then set up for the night. Everybody worked on get-ins, which became faster and easier the more we did. Then a quick tech, for lighting and sound levels, then a short company talk about any changes, new verses, new jokes, etc, for that night or that place. We rehearsed the changes, checked props and costumes, and if we were lucky found the digs or some fish and chips. The show went up at eight. Some liked to be in at seven, to get organised. Others spent the time in the pub, getting to know the audience, turning up alarmingly near time to start. By eight Allan was fiddling, the company chatting to the audience or finally sorting out their gear, and when it felt right, we began. The show was two hours long, with no interval. There was generally nowhere to go in an interval, and the disruption not worth it. We had planted sections of the show in various places that made up for the lack of a break, and nobody ever complained. One old lady of 87 actually told us it was too short.

At the end of the show, everybody struck their own costumes and props, I did my roadie bit with the band while the stage was

New methods of gauging audience response — John McGrath and the boys

dismantled and the chairs shoved away and the floor swept. In twenty minutes the dance was under way. Allan had an ability to get pissed during those twenty minutes that was unnatural. Everybody needed something to charge up their batteries for the three or four hours ahead. The dances varied, sometimes terrific, sometimes thin, but usually enjoyable. We tried to finish at 1.30, but didn't always succeed. During the dances, those not playing in the band packed and wrapped lights, costumes, props, stage, etc, quietly, and at the end, we wrapped the band gear, and everything was ready for loading the next morning. We were generally invited to somebody's place after the dance and the intrepid went for a wind-down with a few quite songs, a chat and a cup of tea. Our children slept in the same room as us, and were looking for life and adventure soon after eight the next morning, so Liz and I resigned ourselves to a reputation for anti-social pit-seeking most nights, though not all. By ten, everybody was back at the hall to load, and wearily did so, and after a few groans, we were off again, hairs of dogs bristling, with blood-orange eyes. It's a great way to shatter your constitution.

We had Sundays and Mondays off, and usually made for Rogart on the east or Dornie on the west, supposedly to rest and recover, though somehow Allan's fiddle or Doli's singing would draw them into the local, and another, more impromptu, ceilidh would be under way. All found it a physical strain, some found it a social strain as well. Constantly in public, always aware of representing the company, always involved in arguments — historical, political, social, economic. But it was never less than rewarding, because of the nature of the people we were amongst — who gave us more than we could ever give them in every way.

The company held together as people under these conditions, of over-work, relentlessly being thrown together, no privacy and constant reworking, rewriting and re-rehearsal, astonishingly well. One minor incident, when one got angry with another for being pissed and a bit casual during the show and said so on stage, could have blown up, but a long and painful company meeting sorted that out, and a lot of things looming on the horizon as well. We were very happy, had no time for jealousies, spites and gossip, and were bound together by a common purpose, which was being triumphantly achieved. If any polarisation took place it was the inevitable one, between those with strong political responsibility which was taken as earnestness and commissaring, and those with strong responsibilities to entertaining and pleasing the audience, which were taken as ego-boosting and copping out. But these were not real divisions in any way, though they grew to seem so many months later. The politicos were every bit as entertaining and the entertainers as deeply concerned, in fact. It

Allan Ross, John McGrath, David MacLennan: 'But will it fit in the van?'

was only in discussion away from work that these seemed like divisions of any importance. The most striking thing was that I had never known a company with as much respect for one another, or as much ability to criticise one another constructively, as this one.

* * *

We did our last show of the Highland tour at Bonar Bridge, then set off south on the long drive to Oban. Billy Wolfe, the Chairman of the Scottish Nationalist Party, had seen the show and invited us to perform at an evening's entertainment he was giving to delegates after the party's annual conference. We wrote pointing out that we were not nationalists, and would attack bourgeois nationalism, but he repeated the invitation, hoping our politics would stimulate discussion within his party. We discussed it, and decided to go. There are many socialists in the SNP, who are there for lack of any other party that is not run from London. And it would do no harm for the chauvinists and tartan Tories to get a dose of what we were saying. We were attacked by comrades on the left for going at all, but they didn't know why we went, or what effect we had, had not read James Connolly or John Maclean, or even, as far as I could tell, Lenin on 'The Right of Nations to Self Determination', so we left them to their sectarian thunderings and got on with it.

The hall was enormous, the stage a thin slit half a mile from the back and the acoustics dreadful. We had all of half an hour to sort it out, lighting and all, but we did, and it worked. Reactions differed from various parts of the hall. I shall never forget Liz squaring up to all 500 of them and delivering 'Nationalism is not enough. The enemy of the Scottish people is Scottish capital as much as the foreign exploiter' — with shattering power. Some cheered, some booed, the rest were thinking about it.

At the end, a ten minute standing ovation, and the company responding with raised fists and a short speech about socialism and nationalism. It was worth doing, and right to do it. We loaded again, and drove off through the night to Edinburgh, aching with tiredness, happy.

* * *

At Cumbernauld a small posse of BBC men came riding out to track down some of our outlaw actors. They ended up taking

on the whole show. After many a hassle, John Mackenzie finally
filmed a version of it, which has now been shown on BBC-TV's
Play for To-day twice and sold all over the world.

*　　*　　*

We had had so many demands from places we hadn't been able
to play in for us to come, and so many from places we had
visited to come back again, that a second tour in the autumn
was virtually fixed up before we left. And we wanted to come
back. For our own pleasure, for the friends we had made, and
for the political work the play was doing.

After filming the TV version, we rehearsed the show in
Edinburgh, and set off again, for another six weeks in the
Highlands, during which time only three or four shows were not
completely sold out. Then two weeks in the Glasgow Citizens',
a week in Ayrshire, and a final fortnight in the Lyceum,
Edinburgh. We had to adapt the show a certain amount for the
big theatres, but the size, enthusiasm and nature of the Glasgow
and Edinburgh audiences made it worth the changes, and the
spirit of the show was much the same. And it meant a great deal,
particularly in Glasgow, whose people were nearly all driven off
their land, Scottish or Irish, and who are now demonstrably at
the mercy of the whims of capitalism. Had UCS (Upper Clyde
Shipbuilders) closed, they would have been cleared yet again.
They knew what we were talking about, and gave us plenty back.

The theatre can never *cause* a social change. It can articulate
the pressures towards one, help people to celebrate their
strengths and maybe build their self-confidence. It can be a
public emblem of inner, and outer, events, and occasionally a
reminder, an elbow-jogger, a perspective-bringer. Above all, it
can be the way people can find their voice, their solidarity and
their collective determination. If we achieved any one of these,
it was enough.

*　　*　　*

One thing I had insisted on was that we broke out of the 'lament
syndrome'. Ever since Culloden, Gaelic culture has been one of
lament — for exile, for death, for the past, even for the future.
Beautiful, haunting lament. And in telling the story of the
Highlands since 1745, there are many defeats, much sadness to
relate. But I resolved that in the play, for every defeat, we would

also celebrate a victory, for each sadness, we would wipe it out with the sheer energy and vitality of the people, for every oppression, a way to fight back. At the end, the audience left knowing they must choose, and that now, of all times, they must have confidence in their ability to unite and win. We wanted to go on saying that to people. It couldn't be said too often.

The whole 7:84 Company at Bowmore

The Cheviot, the Stag and the Black, Black Oil was given its first public airing at the 'What Kind of Scotland?' conference in Edinburgh on 31 March 1973, and first performed in Aberdeen at the Arts Centre, then throughout the seven crofting counties and many places in the south of Scotland. The composition of the 7:84 Theatre Company who performed it was as follows:

John Bett	Sellar/Duke/Minister/Whitehall, etc.
John McGrath	Writer/Director, etc.
David MacLennan	Stage Management/Indian/Crofter, etc.
Dolina MacLennan	Gaelic Singer/Janet/Mary MacPherson/ Gaelic tuition, etc.
Elizabeth MacLennan	Old Woman/Lady Phosphate/ HB Stowe/Accordion, etc.
Chris Martin	Stage Management/Admin./Queen Victoria, etc.
Alex Norton	Singer/Donald Macleod/Selkirk/ Polwarth/Roustabout/Guitar/Banjo, etc.
Bill Paterson	M.C./Loch/Sturdy Highlander/ McChuckemup/Texas Jim/Vocals, etc.
Allan Ross	Fiddle/Indian/Crofter/Bass Guitar/ Musicman.

This company worked together on the research, text, presentation and music of the play. They were also the cast of thousands, the Force Ten Gaels Dance Band, and the Nortones Rock Group.

Additional credits:

John Byrne — Pop-up Book
Eileen Hay — Costumes
Ferelith Lean — Administration

The evening begins with THE FIDDLER *playing Scottish and Irish fiddle tunes among the audience, in the bar, foyer, etc., as the audience are coming in. The Company are preparing their props, costumes, etc. at the side of the platform, talking to friends in the audience, playing drum, whistle, etc. to accompany the fiddle; the audience stamp their feet, clap, etc. to the music, if they want to.*

The stage is a platform on the floor of the hall, with four chairs on either side of it, on the floor, the same chairs that the audience are sitting on. There is a microphone centre front, and speakers on either side. Every member of the cast has his or her chair, and all their props, costumes, musical instruments, etc., are arranged by them, in full view of the audience, around their chair, or hanging on nails in walls, etc. behind them.

In the centre of the stage a huge book stands, upright, closed, with the title of the play on the cover.

When the audience is almost all in, and the Company nearly ready and all sitting on stage, the fiddle plays a reel that everybody can stamp their feet to. As it finishes, the M.C. comes on stage, and, after applause for the fiddler, welcomes the audience, comments on weather, conditions in the hall, etc.

Then he proposes to start the evening with a song the audience can all join in, and by special request, it will be: 'These Are My Mountains'.

A brief intro on the fiddle, and the M.C. *leads the audience in the singing. After a few lines, he says we can do better than that, or terrible, or very good, but let's get some help — and says:* 'We've brought some mountains with us — can we have the mountains, please, lads? Go the bens.' *He plays a roll on the drum as the rest of the Company lift the book, lay it flat on the actual stage of the hall or some arrangement to lift it higher than the acting platform, behind it. They open the first page, and, as in children's pop-up books, a row of mountains pops up from in between the pages. The* M.C. *then calls on the words — and two members of the Company hold up a sheet with the words of the song printed on it. He calls up the accordion, and says we're all set, now we can really sing.*

He and the whole Company, with fiddle and accordion, lead a chorus, verse and final rousing chorus of 'These Are My Mountains'.

These Are My Mountains
(words and music: James Copeland)

For these are my mountains
And this is my glen
The braes of my childhood
Will see me again
No land's ever claimed me
Though far I did roam
For these are my mountains
And I'm coming home.

For fame and for fortune
I've wandered the earth
But now I've come back to
The land of my birth
I've gathered life's treasures
But only to find
They're less than the pleasures
I first left behind.

Repeat verse.

M.C. Later on we're going to have a few songs like that one — if you know the words, join in — and then we're going to have a dance, and in between we'll be telling a story. It's a story that has a beginning, a middle, but, as yet, no end —

GAELIC SINGER (*begins to sing a quiet Jacobite song in Gaelic*).
Och! a Thearlaich òig Stiubhairt,
Is e do chùis rinn mo leir eadh,
Thug thu bhuam gach ni bh'agam,
Aun au cogadh na t-aobhar:
Cha chrodh, a's cha chaoirich —

M.C. It begins, I suppose, with 1746 — Culloden and all that. The Highlands were in a bit of a mess. Speaking — or singing — the Gaelic language was forbidden. (*Singing stops.*) Wearing the plaid was forbidden. (SINGER *takes off her plaid, sits.*)

Dolina MacLennan, the Gaelic singer

Things were all set for a change. So Scene One — Strathnaver 1813.

Drum Roll. Page of book turned, a cottage pops up from in between the next two pages.

Enter two Strathnaver girls, singing.

GIRLS. Hé mandu's truagh nach tigeadh
Hé mandu siod 'gam iarraidh
Hé mandu gille's litir
He ri oro each is diollaid
Heman dubh hi ri oro
Hó ró hù ó

As they sing, a YOUNG HIGHLANDER *comes on, watches them, talks to audience.*

Y.H. The women were great at making it all seem fine. But it was no easy time to be alive in. Sir John Sinclair of Caithness had invented the Great Sheep; that is to say, he had introduced the Cheviot to the North. Already in Assynt the Sutherland family had cleared the people off their land — and the people were not too pleased about it.

FIRST WOMAN. Ach blethers —

SECOND WOMAN. Cha chuir iad dragh oirnne co diubh. (They

won't bother us here).

FIRST WOMAN. The Countess has always been very kind to us.

Y.H. Aye, and she's away in England.

FIRST WOMAN. Why wouldn't she be?

Y.H. With her fancy palaces and feasts for Kings and fine French wines — and it's our rent she's spending.

FIRST WOMAN. Rent! You never pay any rent —

Y.H. Where would I get the money to pay rent? (*To audience.*) If it's not bad weather flattening the barley, it's mildew in the potatoes, and last year it was both together . . . And now they're talking about bringing in soldiers to clear us off the land completely . . .

SECOND WOMAN. Saighdearan? De mu dheidhinn saighdearan? (Soldiers — what do you mean, soldiers?)

Y.H. There were one hundred and fifty of them arrived in a boat off Lochinver.

FIRST WOMAN. Would you get on with some work?

SECOND WOMAN. Seo-lion an cogan. (Here fill up the bucket)

> *They sing on, as* Y.H. *goes to a corner of the cottage to pee in the bucket. They watch him and laugh. Suddenly he panics, does up his trousers and rushes over.*

Y.H. Here — there's a couple of gentlemen coming up the strath.

FIRST WOMAN. Gentlemen?

Y.H. (*to audience*). The two gentlemen were James Loch and Patrick Sellar, factor and under-factor to the Sutherland estates.

FIRST WOMAN. Oh, look at the style of me . . .

Y.H. (*handing them the bucket*). You might find a good use for this. (*Goes.*)

SECOND WOMAN. I hope they have not come to improve us.

FIRST WOMAN. Bi samhach. (Behave yourself). (*Giggles.*)

> *Enter* PATRICK SELLAR *and* JAMES LOCH, *looking very grand.* SELLAR *sniffs the bucket, ignores the women, who are huddled under their shawls.*

*'There's a couple of gentlemen
coming up the strath'*

SELLAR (*with a Lowland Scots accent*). Macdonald has told me,
Mr. Loch, there are three hundred illegal stills in Strathnaver
at this very moment. They claim they have no money for
rent — clearly they have enough to purchase the barley. The
whole thing smacks of a terrible degeneracy in the character
of these aboriginals . . .

LOCH. The Marquis is not unaware of the responsibility his
wealth places upon him, Mr. Sellar. The future and lasting
interest and honour of his family, as well as their immediate
income, must be kept in view.

They freeze. A phrase on the fiddle. Two SPEAKERS
intervene between them, speak quickly to the audience.

SPEAKER 1. Their immediate income was over £120,000 per
annum. In those days that was quite a lot of money.

SPEAKER 2. George Granville, Second Marquis of Stafford,
inherited a huge estate in Yorkshire; he inherited another at
Trentham in the Potteries; and he inherited a third at Lilleshall
in Shropshire, that had coal-mines on it.

SPEAKER 1. He also inherited the Bridgewater Canal. And, on
Loch's advice, he bought a large slice of the Liverpool-
Manchester Railway.

Bill Paterson as James Loch

SPEAKER 2. From his wife, Elizabeth Gordon, Countess of
Sutherland, he acquired three-quarters of a million acres of
Sutherland — in which he wanted to invest some capital.

Another phrase on the fiddle: they slip away.
SELLAR *and* LOCH *re-animate.*

SELLAR. The common people of Sutherland are a parcel of
beggars with no stock, but cunning and lazy.

LOCH. They are living in a form of slavery to their own
indolence. Nothing could be more at variance with the general
interests of society and the individual happiness of the people
themselves, than the present state of Highland manners and
customs. To be happy, the people must be productive.

SELLAR. They require to be thoroughly brought to the coast,
where industry will pay, and to be convinced that they must
worship industry or starve. The present enchantment which
keeps them down must be broken.

LOCH. The coast of Sutherland abounds with many different
kinds of fish. (LOCH *takes off his hat, and speaks directly to*

the audience.) Believe it or not, Loch and Sellar actually used these words. (*Puts hat on again.*) Not only white fish, but herring too. With this in mind, His Lordship is considering several sites for new villages on the East Coast — Culgower, Helmsdale, Golspie, Brora, Skelbo and Knockglass — Helmsdale in particular is a perfect natural harbour for a fishing station. And there is said to be coal at Brora.

SELLAR. You will really not find this estate pleasant or profitable until by draining to your coast-line or by emigration you have got your mildewed districts cleared. They are just in that state of society for a savage country, such as the woods of Upper Canada — His Lordship should consider seriously the possibility of subsidising their departures. They might even be inclined to carry a swarm of dependants with them.

LOCH. I gather you yourself Mr. Sellar, have a scheme for a sheep-walk in this area.

SELLAR. The highlands of Scotland may sell £200,000 worth of lean cattle this year. The same ground, under the Cheviot, may produce as much as £900,000 worth of fine wool. The effects of such arrangements in advancing this estate in wealth, civilisation, comfort, industry, virtue and happiness are palpable.

Fiddle in — Tune, 'Bonnie Dundee', *quietly behind.*

LOCH. Your offer for this area, Mr. Sellar, falls a little short of what I had hoped.

SELLAR. The present rents, when they can be collected, amount to no more than £142 per annum.

LOCH. Nevertheless, Mr. Sellar, His Lordship will have to remove these people at considerable expense.

SELLAR. To restock the land with sheep will cost considerably more.

LOCH. A reasonable rent would be £400 per annum.

SELLAR. There is the danger of disturbances to be taken into account. £300.

LOCH. You can depend on the Reverend David Mackenzie to deal with that. £375.

SELLAR. Mackenzie is a Highlander. £325.

LOCH. He has just been rewarded with the parish of Farr — £365.

SELLAR. I shall have to pay decent wages to my plain, honest, industrious South-country shepherds — £350.

LOCH. You're a hard man, Mr. Sellar.

SELLAR. Cash.

LOCH. Done.

They shake hands, then prepare to sing — 'High Industry' to the tune of 'Bonnie Dundee'.

LOCH & SELLAR.
As the rain on the hillside comes in from the sea
All the blessings of life fall in showers from me
So if you'd abandon your old misery —
I will teach you the secrets of high industry:

Your barbarous customs, though they may be old
To civilised people hold horrors untold —
What value a culture that cannot be sold?
The price of a culture is counted in gold.

Chorus:
As the rain, etc.

Loch and Sellar: 'I will teach you the secrets of high industry'

LOCH. There's a many a fine shoal of fish in the sea
    All waiting for catching and frying for tea —
    And I'll buy the surplus, then sell them you see
    At double the price that you sold them to me.

    Chorus:
    As the rain, etc.

SELLAR. I've money to double the rent that you pay
    The factor is willing to give me my way
    So off you go quietly — like sheep as they say —
    I'll arrange for the boats to collect you today.

    Chorus:
    As the rain, etc.

LOCH & SELLAR. Don't think we are greedy for personal gain
    What profit we capture we plough back again
    We don't want big houses or anything grand
    We just want more money to buy up more land.

    Chorus:
    As the rain, etc.

At the end of the song they go off. The GAELIC SINGER
stands and says:

SINGER. Mo Dhachaidh. (My Home).

*She sings the song, in Gaelic. The Company and audience
join in the chorus.*

SINGER. Seinn he-ro-vo, hu-ro-vo hugaibh o he,
    So agaibh an obair, bheir togail do m' chridhe,
    Bhith stiuireadh mo chasan do m' dhachaidh bheag fhein
    Air criochnachadh saothair an là dhomh.

    Seall thall air an aiseag am fasgadh nan craobh
    Am botham beag geal ud 'se gealaicht le aol
    Sud agaibh mo dhachaidh 'se dhachaidh mo ghaoil
    Gun chaisteal 's an t-saoghal as fhearr leam.

    Chorus:
    Seinn he-ro-vo *etc.*

    'S an ait ud tha nadur a ghnath cur ri ceol,
    Mur e smeorach 's an duilleach 'se'n uiseag neoil
    No caochan an fhuarain ag gluasad troimh lon
    No Morag ri cronan do'n phaisde.

    Final chorus.

At the end of the song, the First Strathnaver GIRL *takes the stage.*

FIRST GIRL. A Poem by Donnachadh Buidhe, the Chisholm bard.

'Destruction to the sheep from all corners of Europe. Scab, wasting, pining, tumours on the stomach and on the hide. Foxes and eagles for the lambs. Nothing more to be seen of them but fleshless hides and the grey shepherds leaving the country without laces in their shoes.
I have overlooked someone. The Factor. May he be bound by tight thongs, wearing nothing but his trousers, and beaten with rods from head to foot. May he be placed on a bed of brambles, and covered with thistles.'

Enter PATRICK SELLAR. *He pats the baby the* FIRST GIRL *is carrying on the head, then walks up to audience.*

SELLAR. I am not the cruel man they say I am. I am a business man.

He winks and goes, leaving the Two Strathnaver GIRLS *on stage. Whistles of warning come from around them. They are alarmed, but not afraid. They call other women's names, shouting to them in Gaelic: Hurry up, get down here, there come the men with the papers.*

OLD MAN *comes on, anxious.*

OLD MAN. Dé tha sibh a' deanamh? (What are you up to?)

FIRST GIRL. A bheil thu bodhar? (Are you deaf?)

SECOND GIRL. Nach eil thu 'gan cluinntinn? (Can't you hear them?)

OLD MAN. De? (What?)

SECOND GIRL. Tha iad a' tighinn le'n cuid pairpearan, air son 'ur sgapadh. (They're coming with their papers to have us thrown out.) Nach eil thu dol a chur stad orra?

OLD MAN. Oh cha chuir iad dragh oirnne co-dhiùbh.

SECOND GIRL. Cha chuir? Gabh dhaibh le do chromag — (Give it them with your stick).

OLD MAN. Na bi gorach — (Och, away).

SECOND GIRL. Mur a gabh thusa gabhaidh mise — (If you won't, I will).

OLD MAN. The Countess of Sutherland will not leave us
without —

FIRST GIRL. Tell that to the people of Eddrachilles.

*She thrusts the baby into his arms. Both women call to the
other women to come and fight.*

SECOND GIRL. Mhairi! Greasaibh oirbh! (Hurry up).

FIRST GIRL. Kirsti! The men are all gone and the ones that are
here are useless!

SECOND GIRL (*to* OLD MAN). Mo naire mhor ort. (Shame on you).

The GIRLS *go out.* OLD MAN *shouts after them.*

OLD MAN. We will form a second line of defence.

He turns to the audience as himself.

When they came with the eviction orders, it was always the
women who fought back . . . Glen Calvie, Ross-shire.

He introduces READERS *from the Company, who stand in
their places and read from books:*

READER 1. 'The women met the constables beyond the
boundaries over the river, and seized the hand of the one who
held the notices. While some held it out by the wrist, others
held a live coal to the papers and set fire to them.'

OLD MAN. Strathoykel, Sutherland.

READER 2. 'When the Sheriff and his men arrived, the women
were on the road and the men behind the walls. The women
shouted "Better to die here than America or the Cape of Good
Hope". The first blow was struck by a woman with a stick.
The gentry leant out of their saddles and beat at the women's
heads with their crops.'

READER 3. In Sollas, North Uist, lands held by MacDonald of the
Isles. 'In one case it was necessary to remove two women out
of the house by force; one of the women threw herself upon
the ground and fell into hysterics, barking and yelling like a
dog, but the other woman, the eldest of the family, made an
attack with a stick upon an officer, and two stout policemen
had great difficulty in carrying her outside the door.'

OLD MAN. And again in North Uist.

READER 4. 'McBain put his men into two divisions, and they
attacked the women on two sides. They drove them along the

shore, the women screaming to their men — "be manly," and "stand up!" Police and women fought on the sand until McBain recalled his officers and the women crawled away to bathe their bloody heads.'

OLD MAN. Greenyards, Easter Ross.

READER 5. 'Sheriff Taylor accompanied by several officers and a police force of about 30 or more arrived at Greenyards, near Bonar Bridge, and found about 300 people, two thirds of whom were women. The women stood in front, armed with stones, while the men occupied the background. The women as they bore the brunt of the battle were the principle sufferers, a large number of them being seriously hurt, the wounds on their skulls and bodies showing plainly the severe manner in which they had been dealt with by the police when they were retreating.

READER 6. 'The police struck with all their force, not only when knocking down but after, when they were on the ground, they beat and kicked them while lying weltering in their blood. Anne Ross, 40, struck on the breast, kicked in the head. Margaret Ross, 18, head split, alienation of mental faculties very perceptible. Elizabeth Ross, 25, knocked down, kicked on the breasts, the batons tore away part of her scalp, shattered frontal and parietal bones. Her long hair, clotted with blood, could be seen in quantities over the ploughed land. Margaret Ross, mother of seven, fractured skull from baton wounds, died later.
Catherine Ross, who came to help the wounded, struck down until she fell in the river.
Grace Ross, felled with a blow on the forehead.
Helen Ross, brought home on a litter, and for the space of eight days could not move her hands or feet.'

OLD MAN. But for every township that fought back, there were many more that didn't. The landlords had an ally in the heart of the community.

Fiddle plays: 'The Lord is my Shepherd'. *The Company hum quietly as one of the actors is dressed as The* MINISTER *and the* OLD MAN *places his pulpit in position.*

MINISTER. Dearly beloved Brethren, we are gathered here today in the sight of the Lord and in the house of the Lord, to worship the Lord and sing His praises, for He is indeed, the

Lord and Shepherd of our souls. Oh you are sheep, sheep who have gone astray, who have wandered from the paths of righteousness and into the tents of iniquity. Oh guilty sinners, turn from your evil ways. How many times and on how many Sabbaths have I warned you from this very pulpit of your wickedness and of the wrath of the Almighty. For I will repay, saith the Lord. The troubles that are visiting you are a judgement from God, and a warning of the final judgement that is to come. Some of you here today are so far from the fold, have so far neglected the dignity of your womanhood, that you have risen up to curse your masters, and violate the laws of the land. I refer of course to the burning of the writs. And everybody here gathered knows to which persons I am referring. There will be no more of this foolishness. Be warned. Unless you repent, you are in great danger of the fire, where there will be much wailing and gnashing of teeth. On that fearful day when God divides the sheep from the goats, every one of us, and particularly those whom I have spoken of today, will have to answer for their flagrant transgression of authority.

He goes off.

OLD MAN. And it worked . . .

SECOND GIRL. Everywhere, except in Knockan, Elphin and Coigeach.

FIRST GIRL *comes on stage and says, to mounting cheers from the others.*

FIRST GIRL. Here the people made a stout resistance, the women disarming about twenty policemen and sheriff-officers, burning the summonses in a heap, and ducking the representatives of the law in a neighbouring pool. (*Big cheer.*) The men formed a second line of defence — (*Groan*) — in case the women should receive any ill-treatment. (*More groans.*) They, however, never put a finger on the officers of the law — all of whom returned home without serving a single summons or evicting a single crofter!

A big hooch from the Company, the fiddle strikes up and they leap onto the stage to dance to celebrate this victory, the women leading off.

At the end, all go off except the actor playing the OLD MAN,

The dance to celebrate the victory at Coigeach

who comes to the mike and talks to the audience as himself.

OLD MAN. What was really going on? There is no doubt that a change had to come to the Highlands: the population was growing too fast for the old, inefficient methods of agriculture to keep everyone fed. Even before the Clearances, emigration had been the only way out for some. But this coincided with something else: English — and Scottish — capital was growing powerful and needed to expand. Huge profits were being made already as a result of the Industrial Revolution, and improved methods of agriculture. This accumulated wealth had to be used, to make more profit — because this is the law of capitalism. It expanded all over the globe. And just as it saw in Africa, the West Indies, Canada, the Middle East and China, ways of increasing itself, so in the Highlands of Scotland it saw the same opportunity. The technological innovation was there: the Cheviot, a breed of sheep that would survive the Highland winter and produce fine wool. The money was there. Unfortunately, the people were there too. But the law of capitalism had to be obeyed. And this was how it was done:

Bell ringing. Enter SHERIFF'S MAN, *reading eviction order.*

Enter PATRICK SELLAR, *interrupting him.*

SELLAR. Get on with it, man, you're costing me a fortune with your verbiage: I've got a flock of sheep waiting in Culmailly.

SHERIFF'S MAN. Sheriff Macleod said to be sure and read this, Sir —

SELLAR. Macleod's well known to be a poacher — how would he not be sympathetic to other thieves and tinkers? Who's in there, then?

SHERIFF'S MAN. William Chisholm, sir —

SELLAR. Another tinker.

SHERIFF'S MAN. His family have lived here for some time, Mr Sellar —

SELLAR. Well, he'll no be here for much longer — he's a sheep-stealer, a squatter who pays no rent, and the Minister informs me he's a bigamist. Get him out —

SHERIFF'S MAN (*calls at door*). Chisholm! (*From within an OLD WOMAN's voice cries out in terror* — 'Sin Sellar, Sin Sellar!')

SHERIFF'S MAN (*to SELLAR*). There's an old woman in there, sir —

SELLAR. Well, get her out, man!

A WOMAN comes out in great distress. A man, MACLEOD, has come on. He watches.

WOMAN. Mo mhàthair, mo mhàthair. (My mother, my mother).

SELLAR (*annoyed at the Gaelic*). What's she saying?

SHERIFF'S MAN. She says it's her mother, sir —

The WOMAN goes over to him.

WOMAN. O mhaighstir MhicLeoid, tha mo mhàthair ceithir fichead bliadhna 'sa coig deug — 's ma theid a carachadh theid a mort. (Oh, Mr Macleod, my mother is 94 years old and if she's moved she'll die).

MACLEOD. She says her mother is 94 years old, Mr Sellar, and if she's moved she'll die.

SELLAR (*to SHERIFF'S MAN*). Get her out. (SHERIFF'S MAN *hesitates*.) Do your job, man —

SHERIFF'S MAN. I'd rather lose my job, sir —

SELLAR (*quietly*). Get the torch.

SHERIFF'S MAN *goes out.*

MACLEOD. You have a great hatred for the people of these parts, Mr Sellar.

SELLAR. I am compelled to do everything at the point of the sword. These people here are absolutely a century behind and lack common honesty. I have brought them wonderfully forward, and calculate that within two years I shall have all the Estate arranged.

MACLEOD. Aye, to your own advantage. Have you no shame at what you are doing to these people?

SELLAR. Such a set of savages is not to be found in the wilds of America. If Lord and Lady Stafford had not put it into my power to quell this banditti, we may have bid adieu to all improvement.

MACLEOD. Will you not even give her time to die?

SELLAR. Damn her the old witch, she's lived long enough —

Enter SHERIFF'S MAN *with a torch; he throws it onto the cottage.*

— let her burn.

Sound of fire, fire-effect on cottage, screams, etc. Blackout. Silence. Single spot on WOMAN, OLD WOMAN, *and* MACLEOD.

MACLEOD. Five days later, the old woman died.

Lights up.

SELLAR (*to audience*). I am perfectly satisfied that no person has suffered hardship or injury as a result of these improvements.

The Company go back to their seats, and read short sections of accounts of the Clearances from many different areas of the North. Note: *readings to be selected from the following, according to where the show is being done.*

READER. 'Donald Sage, Kildonan, Sutherland. The whole inhabitants of Kildonan parish, nearly 2,000 souls, were utterly rooted and burned out. Many, especially the young and robust, left the country, but the aged, the females and children, were obliged to stay and accept the wretched allotments allowed them on the seashore and endeavour to learn fishing.'

READER. 'Ardnamurchan, Argyll. A half-witted woman who flatly refused to flit was locked up in her cottage, the door being barricaded on the outside by mason-work. She was visited every morning to see if she had arrived at a tractable state of mind, but for days she held out. It was not until her slender store of food was exhausted that she ceased to argue with the inevitable and decided to capitulate.'

READER. Ross-shire. 'From the estate of Robertson of Kindace in the year 1843 the whole inhabitants of Glencalvie were evicted, and so unprovided and unprepared were they for removal at such an inclement season of the year, that they had to shelter themselves in a church and a burying ground. For months there were 19 families within this gloomy and solitary resting abode of the dead.'

READER. 'Ravigill, Sutherland. The factor, Mr Sellar, watched while the burners tore down the house of John Mackay. His wife, although pregnant, climbed on to the roof and fell through in a desperate attempt to protect her home. Her screams of labour were mingled with the cries of protest of her husband who said "the law of the country must surely have changed for such things to be done with the approval of the Sheriff's Officer and the Factor".'

READER. Strathnaver, Sutherland. 'Grace MacDonald took shelter up the brae and remained there for a day and a night watching the burnings. When a terrified cat jumped from a burning cottage it was thrown back in again and again until it died.'

READER. 'Suisinish, Skye. Flora Matheson, aged 96, who could not walk, was evicted while all the able-bodied men and boys were away south to earn money to pay the rent. Her three grand-children — the oldest aged 10 — helped her to crawl along on her hands and knees until she reached a sheep-cot. They remained there until the following December. Meanwhile her son came home from the harvest in the south and was amazed at the treatment his aged mother and children had received. He was then in good health. Within a few weeks, with the cold and damp, he was seized with violent cramp and cough, his limbs and body swelled, and he died. His corpse lay

across the floor, the wind waving his long black hair to and fro
until he was placed in his coffin. The sick grand-children were
removed from the cot by the Inspector for the Poor. The old
woman was reduced to a skeleton and had no food but a few
wet potatoes and two or three shellfish.'

READER. 'The Island of Rhum was cleared of its inhabitants,
some 400 souls, to make way for one sheep farmer and 8000
sheep.'

READER. 'Knoydart, Inverness-shire. John McKinnon, a cottar
aged 44, with a wife and six children, had his house pulled
down. The ruins of an old chapel were near at hand and parts
of the walls were still standing. There MacKinnon proceeded
with his family. The manager of Knoydart then appeared with
his minions and invaded this helpless family even within the
walls of the sanctuary. They pulled down the sticks and sails
they set up within the ruins, threw his tables, stools, chair and
other belongings over the walls, burnt up the hay on which
they slept, and then left the district. Four times they came
and did the same thing.'

READER. 'In 1811 Rogart in Sutherland had a population of
2,148. By 1911 it was 892.'

READER. 'During the time of the Clearances, the population
of the parishes of Killarow and Kilmenny — in Islay — was
reduced from 7,100 to 2,700. The population of the entire
island was halved.'

READER. 'Ceal na Coille, Strathnaver. The people were pushed
further and further down to the coast. They suffered very
much for the want of houses and threw up earthen walls with
blankets over the top, and four or five families lived like this
throughout the winter while the last of their cattle died. They
were removed as many as four or five times until they could
go no further, unless by taking a ship for the colonies.'

From the middle of the Suisinish reading, the GAELIC
SINGER *has been quietly humming the tune of* 'Soraidh Leis
an ait'. *She now stands and sings:*

SINGER. Soraidh leis an àit',
An d'fhuair mi m'arach òg,
Eilean nan beann àrda,
Far an tàmh an ceo.

M.C. *steps forward.*

M.C. Of all the many evictors, Mr Patrick Sellar was the only one who did not escape the full majesty of the law. He was charged with the murder of three people and numerous crimes at — Inverness High Court.

The Company become a murmuring JURY.

Enter the JUDGE. *They stand, then sit silently.*

Enter PATRICK SELLAR.

SELLAR. Re the charge of culpable homicide, my Lord — can you believe, my good sir, that I, a person not yet cognosed or escaped from a madhouse, should deliberately, in open day, by means of an officer who has a wife and family, burn a house with a woman in it? Or that the officer should do so, instead of ejecting the tenant? The said tenant and woman being persons of whom we have no felonious intent, no malice, no ill-will.

JUDGE. Therefore, I would ask you (the jury) to ignore all the charges except two. One of these concerns the destruction of barns. In this case, Mr Sellar has ignored a custom of the country, although he has not infringed the laws of Scotland. And the second case concerns the burning of the house of Chisholm. And here we are reminded of the contradictory nature of the testimony. Now if the jury are at all at a loss on this part of the case, I would ask them to take into consideration the character of the accused, for this is always of value in balancing contradictory testimony. For here there is, in the first place, real evidence as regards Mr Sellar's conduct towards the sick — which in all cases has been proved to be most humane. And secondly, there are the letters of Sir George Abercrombie, Mr Fenton and Mr Brodie — which, although not evidence, must have some weight with the jury. And there are the testimonies of Mr Gilzean, and Sir Archibald Dunbar — (*Sees him in the audience, waves.*) — hello, Archie. All of them testifying to Mr Sellar's humanity of disposition. How say you?

JURY. Oh, not guilty, no, no, no, etc.

JUDGE. My opinion completely concurs with that of the jury.

JURY *applaud* PATRICK SELLAR.

SELLAR. Every reformer of mankind has been abused by the established errors, frauds and quackery. But where the reformers have been right at bottom, they have, by patience, and by their unabating zeal and enthusiasm, got forward, in spite of every opposition. And so, I trust, will Lord and Lady Stafford, in their generous exertions to better the people in this country.

More applause. Distant humming of 'Land of Hope and Glory'.

SELLAR (*pointing to the mountains, from behind which a giant statue slowly emerges — eventually dwarfing the entire hall*). In lasting memorial of George Granville, Duke of Sutherland, Marquess of Stafford, K.G., an upright and patriotic nobleman, a judicious, kind and liberal landlord; who identified the improvement of his vast estates with the prosperity of all who cultivated them; a public yet unostentatious benefactor, who, while he provided useful employment for the active labourer, opened wide his hands to the distresses of the widow, the sick and the traveller: a mourning and grateful tenantry, uniting with the inhabitants of the neighbourhood, erected *this pillar* . . .

Music turns sour. Statue disintegrates or flies away.

Enter a Victorian GENT.

GENT. And now a poem, by Lord Francis Egerton, in honour of the first Duke of Sutherland:

He coughs politely then performs the poem in a Victorian posturing manner, with vivid gestures — some perhaps a little unlikely.

He found our soil by labour un-subdued,
E'en as our fathers left it, stern and rude;
And land disjoined from land, and man from men,
By stubborn rock, fierce tide, and quaking fen,
His liberal hand, his head's sagacious toil,
Abashed the ruder genius of the soil.
The fen forbore to quake, the ascent was plain,
Huge mounds restrained and arches spanned the main.
He tamed the torrent, fertilized the sand,
And joined a province to its parent land.
Recurrent famine from her holds he chased,
And left a garden what he found a waste.

A poem by Lord Francis Egerton

A stranger from a distant land he came,
But brought a birthright where he chose a name;
And native accents shall his loss bewail,
Who came a Saxon and remained a Gael.

Thank you.

At the end of the poem, the Company applaud politely.

Enter the GAELIC SINGER.

SINGER. A translation of a Gaelic poem in honour of the Duke
of Sutherland:
'Nothing shall be placed over you
But the dung of cattle.
There will be no weeping of children
Or the crying of women.
And when a spade of the turf is thrown upon you,
Our country will be clean again.'

She goes off. Enter HARRIET BEECHER STOWE *in a large
pink bonnet.*

HARRIET B.S. . Good evening. My name is Harriet Beecher
Stowe, and I am a lady novelist from Cincinatti, Ohio. You
may have heard of my *Uncle Tom's Cabin*. (*Confidentially.*)
Well, that was about the negro slaves, and my *new* book —

*'Good evening. My name is
Harriet Beecher Stowe . . .'*

Sunny Memories of a Stay in Scotland — is about your *dreamy* Highlanders. And my dear friend and namesake, Harriet, Duchess of Sutherland — I've been visiting with her you know, at her delightful home in London, Stafford House, and her country home in the Midlands, Trentham House, and her ancestral home Dunrobin Castle, Scotland . . . where was I? Oh yes — well she is a very enlightened, charming lady, and she is known for her undying support of the oppressed people of the world — the negroes, the slaves, Mr Garibaldi's Italians — she thinks they all ought to be treated much nicer. And as to those ridiculous stories about *her,* one has only to be here, moving in society to see how excessively absurd they are. I was associating from day to day with people of every religious denomination and every rank of life, and had there been the least shadow of a foundation for any such accusations, I certainly should have heard it. To my view, it is an almost sublime instance of the benevolent employment of superior wealth and power in shortening the struggles of advancing civilisation.

COMPANY. Baa. Baa. Baa., etc.

They come after her on all fours, bleating. She backs away in some confusion. The SHEEP *sing* 'These Are My Mountains.'

Sound of Indian drums, war-whoops, jungle birds, coyotes, hens, dogs barking. Book turns to an Indian setting. Enter RED INDIANS. *They dance and then freeze.*

Enter LORD SELKIRK *in top hat. He passes between the* INDIANS *to the microphone.*

LORD SELKIRK. I am Lord Selkirk and I have a plan. The people of the glens have become a redundant population. I favour their going where they have a better prospect of happiness and prosperity so long as they are not lost to Britain. The present stream of emigration must be diverted so as to strengthen Britain overseas. My partners and I have recently acquired stock worth just over £12,000 in the Hudson's Bay Company of Canada and Fenchurch Street. It is not a controlling interest, but it is a large interest. Our rivals, the Northwest Company, a collection of Frenchmen, have so far ingratiated themselves with the natives — (*indicates them*) — as to become a serious threat to our trading operations throughout the colony. They are ruthless and unprincipled.

'I am Lord Selkirk and I have a plan'

The only hope for the Hudson's Bay Company is to combine the needs of the Highlanders for land with our own most urgent interest, and settle the place. I had at first thought of settling it with Irishmen, but the Colonial Officer pointed out that a colony made up of people so intractable — not to say wild — was foredoomed and unsuitable for our purposes. So I have acquired a tract of land five times the size of Scotland (*indicates the number*) and several boat loads of sturdy Highlanders. There is no point in placing them on land that is already tamed. They must go to the Red River Valley and curtail the activities of the Northwest Company and their Indian friends.

He strikes a pose at the side of the stage and waits. Exeunt INDIANS *beating their drums.*

Enter STURDY HIGHLANDER *punting up a river. He does elaborate pantomime double take at* RED INDIAN *painted on the set, and punts down to the microphone.*

S.H. (*to audience*). Has anybody here seen Selkirk?

LORD SELKIRK (*from his corner*). I was at that time in my house in London anxiously awaiting news.

S.H. Ah well, since himself is not here we'll have to get on with
the tilling of the land. As you can see by my costume, I'm a
Sturdy Highlander and I've been sent here to till the land for
future generations and for Lord Selkirk. While I'm getting
on with the planting of the brussel sprouts and the runner
beans, I am particularly vulnerable to attack from the rear. So
if any of you should see any of those big Red Indians I've
heard about will you let me know? Will you do that now? I
tell you what, you'd better shout something, let me see, let
me see — I know. *Walla Walla Wooskie.* Will you shout that?
Let's have a practice — after three now, one, two, three —
Walla Walla Wooskie!

*He goes through several attempts to get the audience to join
in until they do, with gusto — then:*

Very good. Smashing. Now I can get on with it.

Enter GRANNY *with shawl carrying baby.*

GRANNY. De? What? What?

S.H. What?

GRANNY. I can't hear, I can't hear!

'Walla Walla Wooskie'

S.H. Oh I forgot to tell you — that's Granny. She can't hear a thing. She's never been the same since the police hit her over the head at Strathnaver. So as well as the shouting of the Walla Walla Wooskie will you all wave your hands. (*He does.*) Then Granny can see, and I can hear, and a quick bash with the cromach and we'll be all right. All right? Let's have a practice.

They all do until he's satisfied.

Great, great.

GRANNY *beams, gives the thumbs up and goes off to sit down.*

On with the planting of the radishes!

He starts to dig the ground, singing to himself, head down. Re-enter INDIANS beating drum, tomahawks raised. The audience shouts 'Walla Walla Wooskie'. The INDIANS run off before the STURDY HIGHLANDER sees them. He accuses the audience of having him on. Repeat this twice. The third time they creep on and after some dodging about, stand towering over him tomahawks raised.

FIRST INDIAN Ug!

SECOND INDIAN. Ug!

S.H. (*into microphone*). Gulp!

Enter outrageous FRENCH NORTHWEST TRADER. He signals the INDIANS to leave. They do, tugging forelocks. He taps S.H.. S.H. collapses thinking it's the tomahawks.

His WIFE and GRANNY rush on and watch with suspicion.

N.W.T. I am Nor-west Tra-der! Oo are you?

S.H. I'm fine, hoo's yersel'?

N.W.T. No no, *what* are you?

S.H. I am a sturdy Highlander and this is my Granny. And this is wee Calum.

He indicates the baby she is carrying still.

N.W.T. (*patting the baby's head*). Thank heaven for little Gaels! I have a très bonne idée!

S.H. What?

'Thank heaven for little Gaels!'

N.W.T. A very good idea — why don't *you* go back home!

S.H. Because we have no home to go back to, this is our home now.

WIFE *and* GRANNY *nod.*

N.W.T. That is where you are very wrong my friend, we have ways of making you leave! Où sont mes peaux rouges — (*To audience.*) Anyone who says walla walla wooskie or the waving of the palms will (*He makes throat-cutting gesture.*) Tonto!

RED INDIAN 1 (*leaps on*). Pronto!

N.W.T. Hawkeye!

RED INDIAN 2 (*leaps on*). Och aye!

The INDIANS *come on and stand menacing the group one on each side.*

N.W.T. These are my little friends. They give me furs, beaver skins, Davy Crockett hats and all the little necessities of life. I give them beads, baubles, V.D., diphtheria, influenza, cholera, fire water and all the benefits of civilisation. These — are my mountains, and you're going home.

S.H. (*clinging to his womenfolk*). I'll have to speak to Lord Selkirk about that.

Exit N.W.T. *with hollow laugh.*

The INDIANS *remain where they are.*

The group huddle and freeze.

LORD SELKIRK. Things are not going well in the Red River Valley.

S.H. (*turning his head*). You can say that again!

LORD SELKIRK. Things are not going well in the Red River Valley. The Governor of the Province seems to have no control over the hooligans of the North-West Company and their half-breed servants. I have complained to the Colonial Secretary. Unfortunately the North-West Company denies our allegations and the Governor will not provide troops to protect the settlers. However — the highlanders are a sturdy breed and accustomed to the hazards of life in the wild so I am sending out another three boatloads.

He exits pleased. The lights change to fire on the encampment. The INDIANS *dance round the family, with scalping gestures while they sink down with wails to the ground.*

Watching out for Indians in the Red River Valley

WIFE *and* GRANNY *remain and hum the song,* 'Take me Back to the Red River Valley', *while* S.H. *rises, crosses to the microphone and narrates:*

STURDY HIGHLANDER (*out of character*). But we came, more and more of us, from all over Europe, in the interests of a trade war between two lots of shareholders, and in time, the Red Indians were reduced to the same state as our fathers after Culloden — defeated, hunted, treated like the scum of the earth, their culture polluted and torn out with slow deliberation and their land no longer their own.

The humming dies away and the mouth-organ takes over quietly.

But still we came. From all over Europe. The highland exploitation chain-reacted around the world; in Australia the aborigines were hunted like animals; in Tasmania not one aborigine was left alive; all over Africa, black men were massacred and brought to heel. In America the plains were emptied of men and buffalo, and the seeds of the next century's imperialist power were firmly planted. And at home, the word went round that over there, things were getting better.

GAELIC SINGER *stands and reads a poem in Gaelic.*

SINGER. Gur muladach mise 'smi seo gun duine idir
a thogas, no thuigeas, no sheineas leam dàn
le durachd mo chridhe soraidh slan leis na gillean
a sheòl thar na linne gu manitoba.

Tha luchd fearainn shaor anns an am so ro ghaolach
air storas an t-saoghail a shlaodadh bho chach.
's bidh innleachdan baoghalt 's a gaidhealtachd daonan
gu fogradh nan daoine 's chuir chaorach nan ait.

Cha labhar mi tuileadh mu euchd nam fear curant
do Bhreatuinn fuar urram 'gach cumasg is spairn
'se daoiread an fhearainn a dh 'fhag sinn cho tana
's gun chuimhne air sebastapol 's manitoba.

Enter two comic-stereotype HIGHLANDERS.

HIGHLANDER 1. Scene 5, Isle of Skye, 1882!

Roll on drums.

HIGHLANDER 2. Now at that time, Lord Macdonald was driving the people down to the shores . . .

HIGHLANDER 1. What shores?

HIGHLANDER 2. Oh, I'll have a wee dram!

Roll on drum.

No, but seriously though, he was having a bit of an altercation about the grazing rights on a little moor . . .

HIGHLANDER 1. A little moor?

HIGHLANDER 2. Oh well, that's very civil of you!

HIGHLANDER 1. Oh, Sandy, you're a great one for the drink.

HIGHLANDER 2. Oh Angus I am that, I am.

HIGHLANDER 1. I tell you what, when I'm dead will you pour a bottle of the Talisker over my dead body?

HIGHLANDER 2. Certainly, certainly, you won't mind if I pass it through the kidneys first.

HIGHLANDER 1 *drives him off. Drum roll.*

HIGHLANDER 1. Scene 5, 1882, Isle of Skye, Glendale.

Enter two Glendale WOMEN in shawls. They cross to read a notice.

Alex Norton as a Skye man

WOMAN 1. De thann. (What's this?).

WOMAN 2 (*reads*) 'We the tenants on the estate of Glendale do hereby warn each other to meet on or about 1 p.m. on 7th Feb. 1882 at Glendale Church, for the purpose of stating our respective grievances publicly' — So they're doing something about it at last — 'in order to communicate the same to our superiors.'

WOMAN 1. De th'ann superiors?

WOMAN 2. Na daoine mhora! (The great ones).

WOMAN 1. Huh.

WOMAN 2. As if they'd listen.

The rest of the Company, as the MEN *of Glendale, enter discussing the meeting.*

OLD MAN. The whole of the bruachs are being emptied to make way for the sheep, as if they hadn't done enough already.

YOUNGER MAN. Aye, all the crofts in Glendale are being split up to make room for those they've thrown off, and the land's being worked to death till it will grow no more.

OLD MAN. No wonder, when half our own seaweed is taken from us and we have to row all the way round the point to

"We the tenants on the estate of Glendale do hereby warn each other . . . "

Dunvegan to buy it at 31 shillings and sixpence a ton, and sometimes he's not even in . . .

YOUNGER MAN. Aye, and the rents are going up forbye.

WOMAN 2. Did you hear, the factor's closed all the shops — he's to open his own meal store and we can only buy from him.

OLD MAN. And it's a helluva long row all the way to Dunvegan . . .

WOMAN 1. And they've stuck up a notice to stop us gathering the driftwood from our own shores.

OLD MAN. And that loch can be very choppy . . .

MAN 3. And do you know the factor has ordered me to shoot my own dog in case he worried the sheep —

OLD MAN. Och what are the sheep worried about, they don't have to row all the way round the point —

YOUNGER MAN. Bith eamh sabhach. (Behave yourself).

MAN 3. Order! Order!

YOUNGER MAN (*addresses them all*). Contrary to the opinion of our noble proprietors set forth in the newspapers, notably

Two Skye men

The Scotsman, known hereabouts as The United Liar, they have shown themselves to have no interest in these parts except for the extraction of greater and greater rents, the removal of the people to all corners of the earth and the subjection of those who remain to the will of their factor. Over the last 60 years, we in Skye have put up with just about every indignity a human being can suffer. They have succeeded because we are divided amongst ourselves. It has been proposed that the people of Glendale should unite to take action altogether as one body. We are all in the same situation. Every man and every township has a grievance.

OLD MAN. Och that's right enough.

YOUNGER MAN. If we go one by one to make separate claims, we know what will happen. It should not fall on any one person to be singled out for the wrath of the factor. We must go altogether, and any punishment will have to be inflicted on all of us.

General agreement.

OLD MAN. Ach well I just don't know about that . . .

YOUNGER MAN. To guard against anyone falling out of the ranks, it has been proposed that we one and all subscribe our names in a book, and pledge ourselves as a matter of honour to stand by any demand we may make.

Cheers.

And until our grievances are met, it has been proposed that we hold back our rent.

WOMAN 2. No trouble at all!

Cheers.

YOUNGER MAN. That way the situation might strike the factor with more urgency.

OLD MAN. I might strike him with urgency myself . . .

WOMAN 2. Where's the book — I'll be the first to sign . . .

YOUNGER MAN *produces a book, gives it to* WOMAN 2. *All sign.*

YOUNGER MAN *comes forward, speaks to audience out of character.*

'. . . we one and all subscribe our names in a book . . .'

YOUNGER MAN. The idea of united action spread. The tenants of a certain Dr. Martin of Borreraig were obliged to sell their fish and their cattle to the laird at his own price, and to give him 8 days' free labour each year, or 2/6d a day in lieu. They have now struck against this labour, and propose to walk in the same paths as the men of Glendale. And in the Braes area of Skye a mighty confrontation was about to take place. Lord Macdonald, in order to settle his vast debts, had already driven out the people from most of his estate. His tenants in the Braes area resolved, like the people of Glendale, to withold their rent until certain of their grievances were met.

Lord Macdonald made up his mind to put the law in force against them and not on any account to yield to their demands. The unfortunate Sheriff Officer, his assistant who also happened to be the factor's clerk and his Lordship's ground officer set out from Portree to serve writs of removal on all the people of the townships of Peinichorrain, Balmeanach, and Gedintaillear.

A SINGER *steps forward and sings, the Company joining in the chorus.*

The Battle of the Braes
(To the tune of the Battle of Harlaw)

A Sheriff from the factor came
And he came down our way
By Lord Macdonald he was sent
To clear us out frae Skye

Chorus:
Oh the battle was long but the people were strong
You should have been there that day

His depute Martin came along
He could not speak nor stand
They'd filled him up with uisque beath
To throw us off our land

Chorus:
Oh the battle, etc.

Oh he had come with fifty men
He could not pass that day
For all the women from the Braes
Went out to bar his way

Chorus:
Oh the battle, etc.

The Laird was angered he was wild
Macdonald must not fail
He sent the sheriff back again
To throw us into jail

Ghorus:
Oh the battle, etc.

And next came fifty policemen
Frae Glasgow they were sent
The Inverness police knew fine
That what we said we meant

Chorus:
Oh the battle, etc.

A wet and dismal morning dawned
As from Portree they rode
The men of the Braes were up in time
And met them on the road

Chorus:
Oh the battle, etc.

All day the cruel battle raged
We showed them we could fight
But five brave men were taken off
To Inverness that night.

Chorus:
Oh the battle, etc.

The judge he found them guilty men
And fined them two pounds ten
In half a minute he was paid
And off they went again

Chorus:
Oh the battle, etc.

Once more Macdonald's anger broke
'Invade the Isle of Skye
Two thousand soldiers, boats and guns
The people must comply!'

Chorus:
Oh the battle, etc.

'Oh if we send one million men'
In London they declared
'We'd never clear the Isle of Skye
The Braes men are not feared.'

Chorus:
Oh the battle, etc.

The police up in Inverness
Demanded extra men
No other town in all the land
Would help them out again

Chorus:
Oh the battle, etc.

So back the Sheriff came to Braes
All Scotland watched him go
Will you clear off Macdonald's land?
The people answered NO

Chorus:
Oh the battle was long but the people were strong
You should have been there that day

At the end of the song, a big 'Heugh!' *And all go off leaving the M.C. on stage.*

M.C. Lord Macdonald was forced, in the interests of his own class, to come to a settlement in the Braes. A victory had been won.

The men of Glendale did not fare so well. A gunboat was sent in, and 3 men were imprisoned for 2 months. But the resistance continued. Two gunboats, a transport ship and a hundred marines were sent in against them. Her Imperial Majesty's Government would move in its own time.

Enter QUEEN VICTORIA. *She waves, and sings:* 'These Are Our Mountains.'

QUEEN VICTORIA. These are our mountains
And this is our glen
The braes of your childhood
Are English again

Queen Victoria: 'We are impressed'

Though wide is our Empire
Balmoral is best
Yes these are our mountains
And we are impressed.

Enter shooting party with large armoury. GHILLIE, LORD CRASK, *and* LADY PHOSPHATE OF RUNCORN.

LADY PH. Her Royal Majesty the Queen is so right about the charm of this divine part of the world, what? Your estates, Lord Crask, abound in brown trout and grouse — what? —

LORD CRASK. Has your Ladyship sampled the salmon?

LADY PH. The rugged beauty hereabouts puts one in mind of the poetic fancies of dear Lord Tennyson — what?

LORD CRASK. Lady Phosphate of Runcorn you are too kind.

LADY PH. Oh listen for the vale profound is overflowing with the sound.

Blast of gunfire.

GHILLIE (*tries to stop them*). No no no no — the beaters are just having their tea.

LADY PH. As one does. What?

LORD CRASK. What?

Goes to fire; GHILLIE *restrains him.*

GHILLIE (*to audience*). That's nothing, you should see him when he's fishing.

LADY PH. How far do your domains extend over this beauteous countryside, Lord Crask?

LORD CRASK. I have about 120,000 acres down that way, but most of it's over that way.

LADY PH. Oh Archie . . . Capital, capital, capital . . .

LORD CRASK. Oh yes I've got bags of that too — 200,000 shares in Argentine Beef, half a million tied up in shipping, and a mile or two of docks in Wapping.

LADY PH. Topping —

LORD CRASK. No Wapping —

LADY PH. What?

John Bett as Lord Krask

*Elizabeth MacLennan as
Lady Phosphate*

LORD CRASK *goes to shoot* — GHILLIE *restrains him.*

GHILLIE. No no no no no.

LADY PH. Your highland air is very bracing — I quite fancy a small port . . .

LORD CRASK. Oh — how would you like Lochinver?

LADY PH. No no no, I mean I'd like to wet my whistle —

LORD CRASK (*waving hand*). We've left a bush over there for that sort of thing . . .

GHILLIE *whistles up the beaters.*

GHILLIE. Any moment now sir . . .

LORD CRASK. Here come the grouse, Lady Phosphate —

LADY PH. What?

LORD CRASK. The grouse —

LADY PH. Oh, how lovely. (*She gets out a sten gun.*) I find it so moving that all over the north of North Britain, healthy, vigorous people are deriving so much innocent pleasure at so little cost to their fellow human beings.

Barrage. GHILLIE *aims* LORD CRASK's *gun up higher, struggles with him.* LADY PHOSPHATE *fires her sten from*

'*Any moment now sir . . .*'

'Here come the grouse'

the hip. Bombs, shells, etc. Barrage ends.

GHILLIE. Oh no — Thon was a nice wee boy.

Music — guitar and mandolin begins. LORD CRASK *and* LADY PHOSPHATE *sing a duet.*

BOTH. Oh it's awfully, frightfully, ni-i-ice,
    Shooting stags, my dear, and grice —
    And there's nothing quite so righ-it-it
    As a fortnight catching trite:

    And if the locals should complain,
    Well we can clear them off again.

LADY PH. We'll clear the straths

LORD CRASK. We'll clear the paths

LADY PH. We'll clear the bens

LORD CRASK. We'll clear the glens

BOTH. We'll show them we're the ruling class.

Repeat from: 'We'll clear the straths'. *Instrumental half verse.*

LORD CRASK (*speaking over the music*). Oh they all come here, you know — Lady Phosphate of Runcorn — her husband's big in chemicals — she has a great interest in Highland culture.

'Oh they all come here, you know'

LADY PH. How I wish that I could paint —
    For the people are so quaint
    I said so at our ceilidh
    To dear Benjamin Disraeli.
    Mr. Landseer showed the way —
    He gets commissions every day —
    The Silvery Tay.

LORD CRASK. The Stag at Bay

LADY PH. The misty Moor —

LORD CRASK. Sir George McClure

BOTH. We are the Monarchs of the Glen —

LADY PH. The Shepherd Boy

LORD CRASK. Old Man of Hoy

LADY PH. And Fingal's Cave

LORD CRASK. The Chieftain Brave

BOTH. We are the Monarchs of the Glen

LORD CRASK. We love to dress as Highland lads
    In our tartans, kilts and plaids —

LADY PH. And to dance the shean trew-oo-oos
    In our bonnie, ghillie, shoes —

BOTH. And the skirling of the pi-broch
  As it echoes o'er the wee-loch

LORD CRASK. We love the games

LADY PH. Their funny names

LORD CRASK. The sporran's swing

LADY PH. The Highland fling.

BOTH. We are more Scottish than Scotch.

LADY PH. The Camera-ha

LORD CRASK. The Slainte-Vah

LADY PH. Is that the lot?

BOTH. Sir Walter Scott —
  We are more Scottish than the Scotch.

They become more serious. They turn their guns on the audience.

LORD CRASK. But although we think you're quaint,
  Don't forget to pay your rent,
  And if you should want your land,
  We'll cut off your grasping hand.

LADY PH. You had better learn your place,
  You're a low and servile race —
  We've cleared the straths

LORD CRASK. We've cleared the paths

LADY PH. We've cleared the bens

LORD CRASK. We've cleared the glens

BOTH. And we can do it once again —

LADY PH. We've got the brass

LORD CRASK. We've got the class

LADY PH. We've got the law

BOTH. We need no more —
  We'll show you we're the ruling class.

Song ends.

GHILLIE. You're in fine voice today Lord Crask and Lady Phosphate.

LORD CRASK. Thank you, MacAlister —

GHILLIE. Er — MacPherson, sir —

LORD CRASK. Yes, that's right MacDougall. Do you know, Lady Phosphate, there's a whole lot of trouble-makers, do-gooders, woolly thinkers in the South trying to say these people aren't satisfied in some way or another.

LADY PH. Oh — ghastly . . .

LORD CRASK. Absolute poppycock — look at MacDonald here, he's a bit of a peasant —

LADY PH. Yes, you're a peasant, aren't you?

GHILLIE. MacPherson, sir.

LORD CRASK. Nothing wrong with you is there, Macdonald? No complaints?

GHILLIE. No sir, no sir, not at all.

LORD CRASK. Everything's all right with you, MacAlister —

GHILLIE. Just fine, sir, just fine, everything's just fine.

LORD CRASK. Been with me twenty years. Just like one of the family, aren't you? Mac — er. What's your name again?

GHILLIE. MacPherson, sir.

LORD CRASK. That's right, Mackenzie — none of your people complaining, eh? How's your father?

GHILLIE. Dead, sir —

LORD CRASK. Marvellous, no complaints, marvellous — None of your people had to leave the district, what?

GHILLIE. Oh no sir, my own niece from Skye, Mary, she's away working in your house in Edinburgh — Mary MacPherson's her name.

LORD CRASK. Oh Mary — bright little girl — always singing happily around the house, never understand a word she says.

Exeunt LORD CRASK *and* LADY PHOSPHATE.

GHILLIE. Aye, Mary MacPherson, happy as a lintie, sir.

The GAELIC SINGER *comes on as* MARY MACPHERSON, *sings a very sad song.*

Ged tha mo cheann air liathadh

Le diachainnean is bron
Is Grian mo leth chiad bliadhna
A 'dol sios fo na neòil,
Tha m' aigne air a liònadh
Le iarrtas ro mhòr
Gum faicinn Eilean sgiathach
Nan siantannan 's a' cheò

Ach cò aig a bheuil cluasan
No cridhe gluasad beó
Nach seinneadh leam an duan so
M' an truaighe thainig òirnn?
Na miltean air a' fuadach,
Thar chuan gun chuid gun chòir,
An smaointean thar nan cuantan
Gun Eilean uain' a' cheò.

At the end of the song, the M.C. *comes to the microphone.*

M.C. During the time of the Clearances, many of the men did
not resist because they were away in the Army, defending the
British way of life. By the 1850's, it slowly dawned on people
that they were being used.

*A ridiculous procession, led by bagpipes and drums comes
on, followed by the* 3RD DUKE OF SUTHERLAND. *He
addresses the audience.*

DUKE. Good morning. I have come all this way to Golspie to
speak to you, my tenants, because our country is in need.

TENANT (*from audience*). Baa-aah.

DUKE. The Russians under their cruel despotic Tsar seem to
think they are the masters of Europe. Well, they're not. We
are. And we're going to show him we are. The Queen, God
bless her, upon whose Empire the sun never sets, will not be
dictated to by some pesky, Rusky, potentate. Particularly
when it comes to the great trading arrangements she had made
all over the globe, to the everlasting benefit of all of us, of
you — er — and particularly of me. Now she has called upon
us, her sturdy Highlanders, to come to her aid in far-off
Crimea. In 1800, the 93rd Highlanders was raised, 1000
strong; 800 of them were from Sutherland — tenants of this
estate. They have a long and noble history. They are even
now under orders for Scutari; now we have been asked to
raise the proud banner of the Second Battalion of the 93rd

Highlanders. The Queen needs men, and as always, she looks to the North. My Commissioner, Mr. Loch, informs me that the response so far has been disappointing.

Enter LOCH, *now an old man.*

LOCH. Disappointing? A disgrace. In the whole county of Sutherland, not one man has volunteered.

DUKE. I know you to be loyal subjects of the Queen. I am prepared to reward your loyalty. Every man who enlists today will be given a bounty of six golden sovereigns from my own private purse. Now if you will all step up in an orderly manner, Mr. Loch will take your names and give you the money.

The DUKE *sits. Silence. Nobody moves. The* DUKE *stands angrily.*

DUKE. Damn it, do you want the Mongol hordes to come sweeping across Europe, burning your houses, driving you into the sea? (LOCH *fidgets.*) What are you fidgeting for Loch? Have you no pride in this great democracy that we English — er — British have brought to you? Do you want the cruel Tsar of Russia installed in Dunrobin Castle? Step forward.

Silence. Nobody moves.

The Duke of Sutherland: 'Damn it, do you want the Mongol hordes to come sweeping across Europe . . .?'

For this disgraceful, cowardly conduct, I demand an explanation.

Short silence. OLD MAN *stands up in audience.*

OLD MAN. I am sorry for the response your Grace's proposals are meeting here, but there is a cause for it. It is the opinion of this country that should the Tsar of Russia take possession of Dunrobin Castle, we could not expect worse treatment at his hands than we have experienced at the hands of your family for the last fifty years. We have no country to fight for. You robbed us of our country and gave it to the sheep. Therefore, since you have preferred sheep to men, let sheep now defend you.

ALL. Baa-aa.

The DUKE *and* LOCH *leave.* SOLDIER *beats retreat.*

M.C. One man only was enlisted at this meeting. No sooner was he away at Fort George than his house was pulled down, his wife and family turned out, and put in a hut from which an old female pauper was carried a few days before to the churchyard.

Out of thirty-three battalions sent to the Crimea, only three were Highland.

But this was only a small set-back for the recruiters. These parts were still raided for men; almost as fast as they cleared them off the land, they later recruited them into the Army. The old tradition of loyal soldiering was fostered and exploited with careful calculation.

In the words of General Wolfe, hero of Quebec — 'Some Highland Divisions might be of some use — they are hardy, used to difficult country and no great mischief if they fall.'

They were used to expand the Empire and to subdue other countries, whose natural resources were needed to feed the industrial machine of Great Britain.

Lights go down. Book turns to a war memorial.

Every village has its memorial. Every memorial has its list of men. They died to defend something. Those who came back found very little worth defending.

FIDDLER *plays a lament. At the end the lights go up.*

*On stage, the book changes back to mountains. The Company
stand in a group, out of which an* ACADEMIC *emerges,
wringing his hands plaintively.*

ACADEMIC. If only the Highlands had some resources, things
would be — much better.

M.C.1. The figures of de-population increase and increase.

M.C.2. In 1755, the population of the seven crofting counties
was more than 20% of the population of Scotland.

M.C.3. In 1801 it was 18%.

M.C.4. In 1851 it was 13%

M.C.2. In 1901 it was 7%

M.C.3. In 1951 it was 5%

M.C.4. And yesterday it was 3%

ACADEMIC. If only the Highlands had some resources, things
would be — much better.

M.C.2. In 1861, one hundred and sixty of the islands of the
Hebrides were inhabited. In 1941, there were seventy three.

ACADEMIC *goes to the microphone, holding a book.*

ACADEMIC. All this created a mighty wilderness. In the words
of the Highlands and Islands Development Board Brochure —
Explore the Highlands and Islands: 'A great open lung,
guaranteed to breathe new life into the most jaded . . .
Overcrowding? Not in Sutherland . . . a land of solitary
splendour — mountains, lochs and glens of unrivalled beauty
add a sharper poignancy to the scattered stones of the ruined
crofting townships.' Yes, the tragedy of the Highlands has
become a saleable commodity.

Enter ANDY McCHUCKEMUP, *a Glasgow Property-operator's
man. He looks round, takes the mike.*

ANDY. The motel — as I see it — is the thing of the future. That's
how we see it, myself and the Board of Directors, and one or
two of your local Councillors — come on now, these are the
best men money can buy. So — picture it, if yous will, right
there at the top of the glen, beautiful vista — The Crammem
Inn, High Rise Motorcroft — all finished in natural, washable,
plastic granitette. Right next door, the 'Frying Scotsman'

'Yous've got your Grouse-a-go-go'

All Night Chipperama — with a wee ethnic bit, Fingal's Caff —
serving seaweed-suppers-in-the-basket, and draught Drambuie.
And to cater for the younger set, yous've got your Grouse-a-
go-go. I mean, people very soon won't want your bed and
breakfasts, they want everything laid on, they'll be wanting
their entertainment and that, and wes've got the know-how to
do it and wes have got the money to do it. So — picture it,
if yous will — a drive-in clachan on every hill-top where
formerly there was hee-haw but scenery.

Enter LORD VAT OF GLENLIVET, *a mad young laird.*

LORD VAT. Get off my land — these are my mountains.

ANDY. Who are you, Jimmy?

LORD VAT. Lord Vat of Glenlivet. I come from an ancient Scotch family and I represent the true spirit of the Highlands.

ANDY. Andy McChuckemup of Crammem Inn Investments Ltd., Govan, pleased for to make your acquaintance Your Worship. Excuse me, is this your fields?

LORD VAT. You're invading my privacy.

ANDY. Excuse me, me and wor company's got plans to develop this backward area into a paradise for all the family — improve it, you know, fair enough, eh?

LORD VAT. Look here, I've spent an awful lot of money to keep this place private and peaceful. I don't want hordes of common people trampling all over the heather, disturbing the birds.

ANDY. Oh no, we weren't planning to do it for nothing, an' that — there'll be plenty in it for you . . .

LORD VAT. No amount of money could compensate for the disruption of the couthie way of life that has gone on here uninterrupted for yonks Your Bantu — I mean your Highlander — is a dignified sort of chap, conservative to the core. From time immemorial, they have proved excellent servants — the gels in the kitchen, your sherpa — I mean your stalker — marvellously sure-footed on the hills, your ghillie-wallah, tugging the forelock, doing up your flies — you won't find people like that anywhere else in the world. I wouldn't part with all this even if you were to offer me half a million pounds.

ANDY. A-ha. How does six hundred thousand suit you?

LORD VAT. My family have lived here for over a century; 800,000.

ANDY. You're getting a slice of the action, Your Honour — 650,000.

LORD VAT. I have my tenants to think of. Where will they go? 750,000.

ANDY. We'll be needing a few lasses for staff and that . . .
700,000 including the stately home.

LORD VAT. You're a hard man, Mr. Chuckemup.

ANDY. Cash.

LORD VAT. Done (*Shake.*)

ANDY. You'll not regret it, sir. Our wee company anticipate
about approximately about 5000 people per week coming up
here for the peace and quiet and solitude — not to forget the
safari park.

LORD VAT. On safari; hippos in the loch, tigers on the bens,
iguana up the burns, rhinos in the rhododendrons.

ANDY. The El Hochmagandy Mexican Lounge Bar.

LORD VAT. Racoons on the rocks . . .

ANDY. Racoons? Wait a minute. This is a white man's paradise.

They go off.

The GAELIC SINGER *comes on, singing:*

SINGER. Haidh-o haidh rum
Chunna mis' a raoir thu

(*repeat twice*)

Direadh na staoir' 's a royal

Haidh-o hu-o
Cha ghabh mis' an t-uigeach

(*repeat twice*)

Cha dean e cail ach rudhadh na monach.

Haidh-o hiar-am
Cha ghabh mis' a siarach

(*repeat twice*)

Cha dean e cail ach biathadh nan oisgean

M.C. It's no good singing in Gaelic any more — there's an awful
lot of people here won't understand a word of it.

SINGER. And why not?

*Drum: 2 chords on guitar. Company members come on stage
to answer this question.*

M.C.1. In the 18th century speaking the Gaelic language was forbidden by law.

Chords.

M.C.2. In the 19th century children caught speaking Gaelic in the playground were flogged.

Chords.

M.C.1. In the 20th century the children were taught to deride their own language.

Chords.

Because English is the language of the ruling class.
Because English is the language of the people who own the highlands and control the highlands and invest in the highlands —

M.C.2. Because English is the language of the Development Board, the Hydro Board, the Tourist Board, the Forestry Commission, the County Council and, I suppose, the Chicago Bridge Construction Company.

Chords.

M.C.3. The people who spoke Gaelic no longer owned their land.

M.C.1. The people had to learn the language of their new masters —

M.C.1. A whole culture was sytematically destroyed — by economic power.

2 Chords.

M.C.1. The same people, no matter what they speak, still don't own their land, or control what goes on in it, or what gets taken out of it.

2 Chords. They sit.

M.C. It's no good walking away lamenting it in either language — what have the people ever done about it?

Drum beat begins.

M.C.4. Easter 1882. Angus Sutherland formed the Highland Land League. In 1884 John Murdoch set up the Scottish Land Restoration League. In 1885 five crofters' M.P.s elected to Parliament.

M.C.5. In 1886, Crofter's Commission set up by Act of Parliament.

M.C.4. Rents reduced by 30%, arrears by 60%; security of tenure guaranteed, hereditary rights established —

M.C.5. The landlords retaliated. Trouble flared up on the Duke of Argyll's estate on Tiree. The turret ship Ajax, with 250 marines, was sent to quell a population of 2000.

M.C.4. October 1886, Skye: writs served at bayonet point. Six crofters arrested. A medal was awarded for every crofter captured.

M.C.5. 1887, Lewis. One thousand crofters raided the Park Deer Forest which had been enclosed, and killed 200 deer. A venison feast was held, with a white-haired patriarch saying grace before the roasting stags.

M.C.4. 1887, Assynt, Sutherland. Hugh Kerr, the crofters' leader, took to the hills pursued by the authorities. The women of Clashmore raided the police station at midnight.

M.C.5. 1904, overcrowded crofters from Eriskay made a land raid on Vatersay and broke in new crofts.

M.C.4. 1912, the Pentland Act gave the government power to force landlords to sell their land to the state.

M.C.5. This power was never used. 1921-22, impatient with the new government's inactivity, young men from overcrowded areas made more land raids on Raasay, Skye, the Uists, Stratherick and Lewis.

M.C.4. 1919, Portskerra, Sutherland. 14 ex-servicemen drove their cattle on to Kirkton farm, led by the piper who had played them ashore at Boulogne. Their own crofts were small, none bigger than three acres.

M.C.5. The land had been promised to them by the Duke of Sutherland. When they came back from the war he had sold it to a wealthy farmer named McAndrew.

M.C.4. Legal injunctions were served on them. They resolved to stay put and not to be daunted by threats.

SINGER *moves forward, sings unaccompanied. At final verses, the Company join in, humming and stamping feet.*

SINGER. I will go

I will go
Now the battle is over
To the land
Of my birth
That I left to be a soldier
I will go
I will go

When we went
To that war
Oh the living was not easy
But the laird
Promised land
If we joined the British army —
So we went
·So we went —

Now we're home
Now we're home
The laird has changed his fancy
And he's sold
All our land
To a farmer who's got plenty
Now we're home
Now we're home

With the pipes
At our head
That had lead us into battle
We set off
For the land
That we fought for in the Army
We set off
We set off

Oh you Land-
Leaguer men
Of Raasay, Skye and Lewis
Had you seen
Us that day
You'd have cheered us on to glory
Had you seen
Us that day

Oh the Laird

Had the law
And the police were his servants
But we'll fight
Once again
For this country is the people's
Yes we'll fight, once again.

(*spoken*) And with these buggers, we'll have to —

M.C. And what is happening now?

M.C.2. A whole new culture is waiting to be destroyed.

M.C.1. By economic power. Until economic power is in the hands
of the people, then their culture, Gaelic or English, will be
destroyed. The educational system, the newspapers, the radio
and television and the decision-makers, local and national,
whether they know it or not, are the servants of the men who
own and control the land.

M.C.3. Who owns the land?

M.C. The same families — the Macleods, the Lovats, the Argylls,
the MacDonalds, the Sinclairs, the Crichton-Stewarts, and the
Sutherlands.

M.C.4. Plus the property dealers.

M.C.5. The shipowners.

M.C.3. The construction men.

M.C. The distillers. The brewers. The textile men.

M.C.5. The sauce-makers.

M.C.4. The mustard kings.

M.C.5. And the merchant bankers.

M.C.3. The new ruling class!

Music. Two of the Company sing.

DUO. We are the men
Who own your glen
Though you won't see us there —
In Edinburgh clubs
And Guildford pubs
We insist how much we care:
Your interests

Are ours, my friends,
From Golspie to the Minch —
But if you want your land
We'll take a stand
We will not budge one inch . . .

(*spoken*) The Sporting Estate proprietor . . .

SINGER 1. If you should wish
To catch the fish
That in your lochs are stacked,
Then take your creel
Book, rod and reel
And get your picnic packed.
Now cast away
The livelong day
But don't think it's all free
You own your rods
The rain is God's
But the rest belongs to me!

(*spoken*) Doctor Green of Surrey . . .

SINGER 2. Doctor Green of Surrey
Is in no hurry
For a ferry to cross the Sound
You want a pier?
Oh no, not here —
I need that patch of ground:
This island she
Belongs to me
As all you peasants know —
And I'm quite merry
For I need no ferry
As I never intend to go.

(*spoken*) The Ministry of Defence . . .

SINGER 1. The Minister of Defence
He is not dense
He knows just what he's found
The place to test
Torpedoes best,
Is right up Raasay Sound
A few bombs too
In a year or two

You can hear the people groan —
This water's ours
So NATO powers
Go test them up your own.

(*spoken*) Continental Tour Operators . . .

SINGER 2. Herr Heinrich Harr
Says it is wunderbar
To shoot animals is it not?
For a reasonable sum
You can pepper their bum
With bullets and buckshot:
You may call us krauts
Cos we're after your trouts
But listen you Scottish schwein —
This is part of a plan
That first began
In nineteen thirty-nine.

DUO. We are the men
Who own your glen
Though you won't see us there.
In Edinburgh clubs
And Guildford pubs
We insist how much we care —
Your interests
Are ours, my friends
From Golspie to the Minch —
But if you want your land
We'll take a stand
We will not budge one inch.

Song ends.

M.C. One thing's for certain, these men are not just figures of fun. They are determined, powerful and have the rest of the ruling class on their side. Their network is international.

M.C.4. Question: What does a meat-packer in the Argentine, a merchant seaman on the high seas, a docker in London, a container-lorry driver on the motorways, have in common with a crofter in Lochinver?

M.C. Nothing at all.

M.C.4. Wrong. They are all wholly-owned subsidiaries of the Vestey Brothers.

M.C. Ah! The Vesteys — owners of over 100,000 acres in Sutherland and Wester Ross! — and directors of approximately 127 companies, including:

M.C.4. Red Bank Meatworks
Monarch Bacon
Blue Star Line
Booth's Steamship Company
Shipping and Associated Industries
Premier Stevedoring
Aberdeen Cold Storage
International Fish
Norwest Whaling
Commercial Properties
Albion Insurance
Assynt Minerals
Assynt Trading
Lochinver Ice and Scottish-Canadian Oil and Transportation.

Music: 'Grannie's Hielan' Hame' *on accordion.*

Enter TEXAS JIM, *in 10-gallon hat. He greets the audience fulsomely, shakes hands with the front row, etc.*

TEXAS JIM (*to the backing of the accordion*). In those far-off days of yore, my great-great grand-pappy Angus left these calm untroubled shores to seek his fortune in that great continent across the Atlantic Ocean. Well, he went North, and he struck cold and ice, and he went West, and he struck bad times on the great rolling plains, so he went South, and he struck oil; and here am I, a free-booting oil-man from Texas, name of Elmer Y. MacAlpine the Fourth, and I'm proud to say my trade has brought me back to these shores once more, and the tears well in my eyes as I see the Scottish Sun Sink Slowly in the West behind. . . . (*Sings.*)

My Grannie's Hielan' Hame.

Blue grass guitar in, country style. He changes from nostalgia to a more aggressive approach.

For these are my mountains
And this is my glen
Yes, these are my mountains
I'll tell you again —
No land's ever claimed me

Though far I did roam
Yes these are my mountains
And I — have come home.

Guitar continues: he fires pistol as oil rigs appear on the mountains.

Fiddle in for hoe-down. Company line up and begin to dance hoe-down.

JIM *shakes hands with audience, then back to mike and begins square dance calls:*

TEXAS JIM. Take your oil-rigs by the score,
Drill a little well just a little off-shore,
Pipe that oil in from the sea,
Pipe those profits — home to me.

I'll bring work that's hard and good —
A little oil costs a lot of blood.

Your union men just cut no ice
You work for me — I name the price.

So leave your fishing, and leave your soil,
Come work for me, I want your oil.

Screw your landscape, screw your bays
I'll screw you in a hundred ways —

Texas Jim: 'I have come home'

*'I'll screw you in a
hundred ways'*

Take your partner by the hand
Tiptoe through the oily sand

Honour your partner, bow real low
You'll be honouring me in a year or so

I'm going to grab a pile of dough
When that there oil begins to flow

I got millions, I want more
I don't give a damn for your fancy shore

1 2 3 4 5 6 7
All good oil men go to heaven

8 9 10 11 12
Billions of dollars all to myself

13 14 15 16
All your government needs is fixing

17 18 19 20
You'll get nothing, I'll get plenty

21 22 23 24
Billion billion dollars more

25 26 27 28
Watch my cash accumulate

As he gets more and more frenzied, the dancers stop and look at him.

27 28 29 30
You play dumb and I'll play dirty

All you folks are off your head
I'm getting rich from your sea bed

I'll go home when I see fit
All I'll leave is a heap of shit

You poor dumb fools I'm rooking you
You'll find out in a year or two.

He stops, freaked out. The dancers back away from him.
He gets himself under control and speaks to the audience.

Our story begins way way back in 1962. Your wonderful government went looking for gas in the North Sea, and they struck oil.

Guitar.

Well, they didn't know what to do about it, and they didn't believe in all these pesky godless government controls like they do in Norway and Algeria and Libya, oh, my God — no, you have a democracy here like we do — so your government gave a little chance to honest God-fearing, anti-socialist businessmen like myself —

Guitar.
Two Company members stand in their places to speak.

M.C.1. Shell-Esso of America, Transworld of America, Sedco of America, Occidental of America — and of Lord Thompson.

M.C.2. Conoco, Amoco, Mobil, Signal.

TEXAS JIM. All of America.

M.C.1. And British Petroleum —

TEXAS JIM. A hell of a lot of American money, honey.

Guitar.
Enter WHITEHALL, a worried senior Civil Servant.

WHITEHALL. You see we just didn't have the money to squander on this sort of thing.

TEXAS JIM. That's my boy —

WHITEHALL. And we don't believe in fettering private
enterprise: after all this is a free country.

TEXAS JIM. Never known a freer one.

WHITEHALL. These chaps have the know how, and we don't.

TEXAS JIM. Yes sir, and we certainly move fast.

M.C.1. By 1963 the North Sea was divided into blocks.

M.C.2. By 1964 100,000 square miles of sea-bed had been handed
out for exploration.

WHITEHALL. We didn't charge these chaps a lot of money, we
didn't want to put them off.

TEXAS JIM. Good thinking, good thinking. Your wonderful
labourite government was real nice: thank God they weren't
socialists.

M.C.1. The Norwegian Government took over 50% of the shares
in exploration of their sector.

M.C.2. The Algerian Government control 80% of the oil industry
in Algeria.

M.C.1. The Libyan Government are fighting to control 100%
of the oil industry in Libya.

Guitar.

WHITEHALL. Our allies in N.A.T.O. were pressing us to get the
oil flowing. There were Reds under the Med. Revolutions in
the middle-east.

TEXAS JIM. Yeah, Britain is a stable country and we can make
sure you stay that way. (*Fingers pistol.*)

WHITEHALL. There is a certain amount of disagreement about
exactly how much oil there actually is out there. Some say
100 million tons a year, others as much as 600 million. I find
myself awfully confused.

TEXAS JIM. Good thinking. Good thinking.

WHITEHALL. Besides if we produce our own oil, it'll be cheaper,
and we won't have to import it — will we?

M.C.1. As in all 3rd World countries exploited by American
business, the raw material will be processed under the control
of American capital — and sold back to us at three or four
times the price —

Texas Jim and Whitehall:
'You'll open your doors to the
oil industry'

M.C.2. To the detriment of our balance of payments, our cost of living and our way of life.

TEXAS JIM. And to the greater glory of the economy of the U.S. of A.

Intro. to song. Tune: souped-up version of 'Bonnie Dundee'. TEXAS JIM *and* WHITEHALL *sing as an echo of* LOCH *and* SELLAR.

TEXAS JIM & WHITEHALL.
As the rain on the hillside comes in from the sea
All the blessings of life fall in showers from me
So if you'd abandon your old misery
Then you'll open your doors to the oil industry —

GIRLS (*as backing group*). Conoco, Amoco, Shell-Esso, Texaco, British Petroleum, yum, yum, yum. (*Twice.*)

TEXAS JIM. There's many a barrel of oil in the sea
All waiting for drilling and piping to me
I'll refine it in Texas, you'll get it, you'll see
At four times the price that you sold it to me.

TEXAS JIM & WHITEHALL. As the rain on the hillside, etc. (*Chorus.*)

GIRLS. Conoco, Amoco, etc. (*Four times.*)

'Conoco, Amoco, Shell-Esso, Texaco . . .'

WHITEHALL.
There's jobs and there's prospects so please have no fears,
There's building of oil rigs and houses and piers,
There's a boom-time a-coming, let's celebrate — cheers —

TEXAS JIM *pours drinks of oil.*

TEXAS JIM. For the Highlands will be my lands in three or four years.

No oil in can.

Enter ABERDONIAN RIGGER.

A.R. When it comes to the jobs all the big boys are American. All the technicians are American. Only about half the riggers are local. The American companies'll no take Union men, and some of the fellows recruiting for the Union have been beaten up. The fellows who get taken on as roustabouts are on a contract; 84 hours a week in 12 hour shifts, two weeks on and one week off. They have to do overtime when they're tell't. No accommodation, no leave, no sick-pay, and the company can sack them whenever they want to. And all that for £27.00 a week basic before tax. It's not what I'd cry a steady job for a family man. Of course, there's building jobs going but in a few years that'll be over, and by then we'll not be able to afford to live here. Some English property company has just sold 80 acres of Aberdeenshire for one million pounds. Even a stairhead tenement with a shared lavatory will cost you four thousand pounds in Aberdeen. At the first sniff of oil, there was a crowd of sharp operators jumping all over the place buying the land cheap. Now they're selling it at a hell of a profit.

Drum. Company step on stage again, speak to the audience.

M.C.1. In the House of Commons, Willie Hamilton, M.P., said he was not laying charges at the door of any particular individual who had *quote:* moved in sharply to cash-in on the prospect of making a quick buck. There is a great danger of the local people being outwitted and out-manoeuvred by the Mafia from Edinburgh and Texas . . . end quote.

M.C.2. The people must own the land.

M.C.3. The people must control the land.

M.C.1. They must control what goes on it, and what gets taken out of it.

M.C.3. Listen to this. Farmers in Easter Ross have had their land bought by Cromarty Firth Development Company.

M.C.2. Crofters in Shetland have had their land bought by Nordport.

M.C.1. Farmers in Aberdeenshire have had their land bought by Peterhead and Fraserburgh Estates.

M.C.3. All three companies are owned by Onshore Investments "of Edinburgh."

M.C.2. Onshore Investments, however, was owned by Mount St. Bernard Trust of London and Preston, Lancashire.

M.C.3. A man named John Foulerton manages this empire. But whose money is he handling? Who now owns this land in Easter Ross, Shetland and Aberdeenshire? Whose money is waiting to buy *you* out?

Drum roll.

M.C.1. Marathon Oil?

M.C.2. Trafalgar House Investments?

M.C.3. Dearbourne Storm of Chicago?

M.C.4. Apco of Oklahoma?

M.C.5. Chicago Bridge and Iron of Chicago?

M.C.2. P & O Shipping?

M.C.3. Taylor-Woodrow?

M.C.1. Mowlems?

M.C.2. Costains?

M.C.5. Cementation?

M.C.4. Bovis?

M.C.3. Cleveland Bridge and Engineering.

M.C.2. These people have been buying up the North of Scotland.

TEXAS JIM. A-a, a-a. With the help of your very own Scottish companies: Ivory & Sime of Edinburgh; Edward Bates & Son of Edinburgh; Noble Grossart, of Edinburgh; and the Bank of Scotland, of — er — Scotland.

M.C.4. And the Shiek of Abu Dhabi's cousin who owns a large slice of the Cromarty Firth . . .

M.C.2. Mrs. Cowan, of the Strathy Inn, was offered a lot of money by a small group of Japanese.

TEXAS JIM. What can you little Scottish People do about it?

Silence. Exit TEXAS JIM.

M.C.2. Mr. Gordon Campbell, in whose hands the future of Scotland rested at this crucial period, said:

WHITEHALL *gets up, does nothing, sits down.*

Scottish capitalists are showing themselves to be, in the best tradition of Loch and Sellar — ruthless exploiters.

Enter S.N.P. EMPLOYER.

SNP EMPLOYER. Not at all, no no, quit these Bolshevik haverings. Many of us captains of Scottish industry are joining the Nationalist party. We have the best interest of the Scottish people at heart. And with interest running at 16%, who can blame us?

M.C.2. Nationalism is not enough. The enemy of the Scottish people is Scottish capital, as much as the foreign exploiter.

Drum roll.

Actor who played SELLAR, *and* WHITEHALL *comes on.*

ACTOR (*as* SELLAR). I'm not the cruel man you say I am. (*As* WHITEHALL.) I'm a Government spokesman and not responsible for my actions . . .

TEXAS JIM. I am perfectly satisfied that no persons will suffer hardship or injury as a result of these improvements.

Drum roll.

Short burst on fiddle. JIM *and* WHITEHALL *go to shake hands. Enter between them, in black coat and bowler hat,* POLWARTH — *not unlike* SELKIRK'*s entrance.*

POLWARTH. I am Lord Polwarth, and I have a plan. The present government seems to have no control over the hooligans of the American oil companies and their overpaid government servants, so the government has appointed me to be a knot-cutter, a trouble-shooter, a clearer of blockages, and a broad forum to cover the whole spectrum. However, I am not a supremo. In this way, the people of Scotland — or at least the Bank of Scotland — will benefit from the destruction of their country.

M.C.2. Before becoming Minister of State, Lord Polwarth was

Whitehall: 'I am a Government spokesman and not responsible for my actions'

Governor of the Bank of Scotland, Chairman of the Save and Prosper Unit Trust, a Director of I.C.I. and was heavily involved in British Assets Trust, Second British Assets Trust and Atlantic Assets Trust, which at that time owned fifty per cent of our old friend, Mount St. Bernard Trust.

Musical intro. Tune: 'Lord of the Dance'.

TEXAS JIM *and* WHITEHALL *turn* LORD POLWARTH *into a puppet by taking out and holding up strings attached to his wrists and back. They sing:*

ALL. Oil, oil, underneath the sea,
    I am the Lord of the Oil said he,
    And my friends in the Banks and the trusts all agree,
    I am the Lord of the Oil — Tee Hee.

POLWARTH. I came up from London with amazing speed
    To save the Scottish Tories in their hour of need:
    The people up in Scotland were making such a noise,
    That Teddy sent for me, 'cos I'm a Teddy-boy . . .

ALL. Oil, oil, etc.

POLWARTH. Now all you Scotties need have no fear,
    Your oil's quite safe now the trouble-shooter's here,
    So I'll trust you, if you'll trust me,
    'Cos I'm the ex-director of a trust company.

Lord Polwarth: 'I am the Lord of the Oil said he'

ALL. Oil, oil, etc.

POLWARTH. Now I am a man of high integrity,
Renowned for my complete impartiality,
But if you think I'm doing this for you,
You'd better think again 'cos I'm a businessman too —

ALL. Oil, oil, etc.

At the end of the song, LORD POLWARTH *freezes.* TEXAS
JIM *and* WHITEHALL *let go of his strings, and he collapses.*
M.C.2. *catches him on her shoulder and carries him off.* JIM
and WHITEHALL *congratulate each other, then turn to the
audience.*

TEXAS JIM. And the West is next in line.

WHITEHALL. And the West is next in line.

GAELIC SINGER. And the West is next in line. Even now
exploration is going on between the Butt of Lewis and the
coast of Sutherland.

WHITEHALL. Don't worry it will take at least five years.

GAELIC SINGER. They've started buying land already.

WHITEHALL. We can't interfere with the free play of the market.

TEXAS JIM. Leave it to me, I'll take it out as quick as I can and
leave you just as I found you.

GAELIC SINGER. Worse, by all accounts.

WHITEHALL. Now look here, we don't want you people
interfering and disturbing the peace — What do you know
about it?

GAELIC SINGER. We'd like to know a hell of a lot more . . .
(*Exit.*)

WHITEHALL. As our own Mr. Fanshaw of the H.I.D.B. said:
'These oil rigs are quite spectacular. I hear they actually
attract the tourists — '

Enter CROFTER *and his* WIFE.

You can give them bed and breakfast.

Doorbell rings.

WIFE. Get your shoes on, that'll be the tourists from Rotherham,

Yorks, and put some peats on top of that coal — they'll think we're no better than theirselves.

CROFTER. Aye, aye, aye — go you and let them in . . .

WIFE. Put off that television and hunt for Jimmy Shand on the wireless.

CROFTER mimes this action.

Oh God, there's the Marvel milk out on the table, and I told them we had our own cows —

Bell rings again.

CROFTER. Aye, aye, aye, they'll be looking like snowmen stuck out there in this blizzard —

WIFE. Och, it's terrible weather for July —

CROFTER. It's not been the same since they struck oil in Loch Duich.

WIFE. Now is everything right?

She wraps a shawl round her head; he rolls up his trouser leg, and throws a blanket round himself to look like a kilt, and puts on a tammy.

WIFE. Get out your chanter and play them a quick failte.

CROFTER. How many would you like?

WIFE. Just the one —

He plays a blast of 'Amazing Grace'. *She takes a deep breath, and opens the door. The visitors are mimed.*

WIFE. Dear heart step forward, come in, come in. (*Clicks fingers to* CROFTER.)

CROFTER (*brightly*). Och aye!

WIFE. You'll have come to see the oil-rigs — oh, they're a grand sight right enough. You'll no see them now for the stour, but on a clear day you'll get a grand view if you stand just here —

CROFTER. Aye, you'll get a much better view now the excavators digging for the minerals have cleared away two and a half of the Five Sisters of Kintail.

WIFE. You'll see them standing fine and dandy, just to the west of the wee labour camp there —

CROFTER. And you'll see all the bonnie big tankers come steaming up the loch without moving from your chair —

WIFE. You'll take a dram? Get a wee drammie for the visitors —

CROFTER. A what?

WIFE. A *drink*. I doubt you'll have anything like this down in Rotherham, Yorks. All the people from England are flocking up to see the oil-rigs. It'll be a change for them.

CROFTER. Here, drink that now, it'll make the hairs on your chest stick out like rhubarb stalks.

WIFE. When the weather clears up, you'll be wanting down to the shore to see the pollution — it's a grand sight, right enough.

CROFTER. Aye, it's a big draw for the tourists: they're clicking away at it with their wee cameras all day long.

WIFE. Or you can get Donnie MacKinnon to take you in his boat out to the point there, to watch the rockets whooshing off down the range — but he'll no go too far, for fear of the torpedoes. Himself here would take you but he gave up the fishing a while back.

CROFTER. It's no safe any more with the aerial bombs they're testing in the Sound. Anyway all the fish is buggered off to Iceland.

WIFE. What does he do now? Oh, well, he had to get a job on the oil-rigs.

CROFTER. Oh, aye, it was a good job, plenty money . . .

WIFE. He fell down and shattered his spine from carelessness. (*Clicks her fingers at him.*)

CROFTER (*brightly*). Och aye!

WIFE. And now he can't move out of his chair. But he has a grand view of the oil-rig to give him something to look at, and helping me with the visitors to occupy him.

CROFTER. No, no, no compensation —

WIFE. But we'll have plenty of money when we sell the croft to that nice gentleman from Edinburgh.

CROFTER. Aye, he made us an offer we can't refuse.

WIFE. And we can't afford to live here any more with the price of things the way they are, and all the people from the village gone, and their houses taken up . . .

CROFTER. We were wondering now about the price of houses in Rotherham.

WIFE. Or maybe a flat. I've always wanted to live in a flat. You'll get a grand view from high up.

CROFTER (*taking off funny hat*). One thing's certain, we can't live here.

WIFE (*very sadly*). Aye, one thing's certain. We can't live here.

The GAELIC SINGER *comes forward; they stay sitting. She sings the verse of* 'Mo Gachaidh'. *The rest of the Company comes on to join the chorus.*

At the end of the song, all stay on stage and speak to the audience in turn.

The people do not own the land.

The people do not control the land.

Any more than they did before the arrival of the Great Sheep.

In 1800 it was obvious that a change was coming to the Highlands.

It is obvious now that another change is coming to the Highlands.

Then as now, the economy was lagging behind the development of the rest of the country.

Then as now, there was capital elsewhere looking for something to develop.

In those days the capital belonged to southern industrialists.

Now it belongs to multi-national corporations with even less feeling for the people than Patrick Sellar.

In other parts of the world — Bolivia, Panama, Guatemala, Venezuela, Brazil, Angola, Mozambique, Nigeria, Biafra, Muscat and Oman and many other countries — the same corporations have torn out the mineral wealth from the land. The same people always suffer.

Then it was the Great Sheep.

Now it is the black black oil.

Then it was done by outside capital, with the connivance of the local ruling class and central government —

And the people had no control over what was happening to them.

Now it is being done by outside capital, with the connivance of the local ruling class and central government.

Have we learnt anything from the Clearances?

When the Cheviot came, only the landlords benefited.

When the Stag came, only the upper-class sportsmen benefited.

Now the Black Black Oil is coming. And must come. It could benefit everybody. But if it is developed in the capitalist way, only the multi-national corporations and local speculators will benefit.

At the time of the Clearances, the resistance failed because it was not organised. The victories came as a result of militant organisation — in Coigeach, The Braes, and the places that formed Land Leagues. We too must organise, and fight — not with stones, but politically, with the help of the working class in the towns, for a government that will control the oil development for the benefit of everybody.

Have we learnt anything from the Clearances? In the 1890's Mary MacPherson, whose family was cleared from Skye, wrote this song:

GAELIC SINGER (*sings*). Cuimhnichibh gur sluagh sibh
Is cumaibh suas 'ur coir
Tha beairteas bho na cruachan
Far an d'fhuair sibh arach og
Tha iarrann agus gual ann
Tha luaidhe ghlas is or
Thameinnean gu 'ur buannachd
An Eilean Uaine a 'Cheo.

M.C. The song says:
'Remember that you are a people and fight for your rights —
There are riches under the hills where you grew up.
There is iron and coal there grey lead and gold there —
There is richness in the land under your feet.

Remember your hardships and keep up your struggle
The wheel will turn for you
By the strength of your hands and hardness of your fists.
Your cattle will be on the plains
Everyone in the land will have a place
And the exploiter will be driven out.'

COMPANY. Cuimhnichibh ur cruadal
Is cumaibh suas ur sroill,
Gun teid an roth mun cuairt duibh
Le neart is cruas nan dorn;
Gum bi ur crodh air bhuailtean
'S gach tuathanach air doigh,
'S na Sas'naich air fuadach
A Eilean Uain a' Cheo.

Articles from the Original Programme

Have the Clearances stopped?

While it is true that the more brutal methods of the past are no longer with us, it is a simple matter to collect the relevant figures to show that even now 150 years after these terrible events began, the western Highlands and islands continue to be cleared. No amount of statistics from the Highlands and Islands Development Board can hide the fact that the talents, the youths, the skills, the ambitions, those who are the lifeblood of scores of communities continue to drain away. For those living in the western seaboard or in the isles figures are unnecessary, they can see it with their own eyes.

It is all too clear, that the method may have changed but the remorseless and insensitive logic of the "improver" remains very much with us. What was once called "improvement" is now called "development," but the touchstone remains profitability not the well being of the community. Last century Strathnaver was exploited for the wealth the land could sustain upon it. This time it is the promise of the wealth contained within it that lures the businessman north. Greed and the profit motive have changed little over the years.

Land means money. The people during the Clearances were forced out of the fertile straths and glens into overcrowded and insanitary townships, on poor ground. They bitterly reflected that even those rocky scraps of land would have been denied them had they held any value for the landlords of the day. The land was poor, to break it in was hard and the only advice that they got was — emigrate. Now, even the land those men broke in in such grim circumstances is wanted, to be restocked with tourists and white settlers. Once again the only advice given is: adapt and put up with it or else — emigrate. The "improvers" of yesterday are the "planners" of today. The message has changed, the attitudes have not.

In 1816, when the appointment of a sheriff was due in Sutherland, the infamous Patrick Sellar wrote: "It is of great consequence that our new Sheriff be no 'Gael' nor 'Mac' — but a plain, honest, industrious *South* countryman."

Sellar has long been in the grave but his ghost remains in the corridors of Westminster and St. Andrew's House. Today it is retired naval flotsam and the jetsam of the colonial office who are appointed to be the servants of the Highlands. They are there to direct the secondary phase of clearance.

What is to be done? The last phase erupted into spirited resistance. From 1820 to 1920 the Highlands reeled to the fight back of the people. Much was achieved by those land leaguers of yesteryear. They taught a lesson to the whole of Scotland as to organisation and resistance. It is a lesson not without relevance today.

Ray Burnett, March 1973.

Some Notes

On the Company

7:84 Theatre Company began work in July 1971. 7:84 was chosen as the name of the group as a means of drawing attention to a statistic published in "The Economist" in 1966 which asserted that 7% of the population of Great Britain owned 84% of the capital wealth. Although this proportion may have fluctuated marginally over the years, we continue to use it because it points to the basic economic structure of the society we live in, from which all the political, social and cultural structures grow. The company opposes this set-up, and tries to present in its work a socialist perspective on our society, and to indicate socialist alternatives to the capitalist system that dominates all our lives today.

After two years' work touring around England, Scotland and Wales, the company decided that, while the London-based company should continue working in England and Wales, three of its founder-members, John McGrath, Elizabeth MacLennan and David MacLennan should contact other Scottish actors, musicians and theatre-workers interested in doing the same kind of work in Scotland. Very soon, 7:84 Theatre Company (Scotland) was formed, and in April 1973, *The Cheviot, the Stag and the Black, Black Oil*, its first production, began its tour of the Highlands. Since then, many new shows, mostly by John McGrath, have been toured round the industrial belt of Scotland as well as the Highlands, and the company have achieved a great international reputation for their work.

On the Play

The Cheviot, the Stag and the Black Black Oil was conceived
in the form of the traditional Highland ceilidh. To tell the story
of the people of the Highlands to the people of the Highlands,
it seemed obvious that the form should be a popular and
traditional one.

Although John McGrath had been working on the idea of the
play, and the historical background to it, for fifteen years, the
whole company was drawn into the process of making it. Each
member checked some areas of research and was free to throw
in ideas, gags, musical suggestions and to question everything
being written. The final result, therefore, represents the talents,
skills and beliefs of the company as a whole.

If other actors decide to perform the piece, they should try
to create the same identification with what they say and do —
something quite different from normal actors' learning of lines.

On the Situation

The people of the Highlands are intensely aware of the tragedy
of their past. They are increasingly aware of the challenge facing
them today. Due to the impersonality and remoteness from
their lives of the decision-making process, some may have come
to see their future as something outside their control, something
pre-determined. This play tries to show **why** the tragedies of the
past happened: because the forces of capitalism were stronger
than the organisation of the people. It tries to show that the
future is **not** pre-determined, that there are alternatives, and it
is the responsibility of everyone to fight and agitate for the
alternative which is going to benefit the people of the
Highlands, rather than the multi-national corporations, intent
on profit. Passive acceptance now means losing control of the
future. Socialism, and the planned exploitation of natural
resources for the benefit of all humanity, is the alternative the
play calls for. Not the "socialism" that merely begs concessions
from capitalism, but the kind that involves every individual in
the creation of the future he or she wants, that measures
progress by human happiness rather than by shareholders'
dividends, that liberates minds rather than enslaving them. Some
will object that this kind of socialism has never been achieved:
this is not true, but even if it were, it is no reason for not fighting
for it.

The Highlands have so much that is good, rare, even unique

in human experience. If the people there, and the working people of the rest of Scotland realise that there is a choice, that it must be made soon, and decisively, then not only can what is good be saved, but a future built in the Highlands, and in the whole of Scotland, that could inspire the rest of the world.

J. McG. June 1974.

Scottish Daily Express — Tuesday 13th February, 1973

Who are in the first division among Scottish landowners? Even the select committee on Scottish Affairs which recently discussed the issue doesn't know for sure. The last official land register was compiled exactly 100 years ago, and experts say it would take exhaustive months and possibly years of research to have it updated. Even if the big landlords were willing to divulge such information — and very few will — it is doubtful if they know themselves down to the last acre just how much they own.

Here we give a 1973 assessment. With so many estates broken up into family trusts and company ownership it could be argued that no one man or woman is the sole proprietor.

Forestry Commission etc.	400,000 acres
The Duke of Buccleugh	338,000 acres
Lord Lovat	200,000 acres
The Earl of Seafield	180,000 acres
The Duchess of Westminster	176,000 acres
Church of Scotland Commissioners	160,000 acres
Cameron of Lochiel	150,000 acres
The Countess of Sutherland	150,000 acres
Lord Burton	141,000 acres
The Duke of Athol	140,000 acres
The Marquis of Bute	117,000 acres
Shipping magnate Ronald Vestey	117,000 acres
Lord Thurso	100,000 acres
The Duke of Argyll	100,000 acres
The Earl of Cawdor	100,000 acres
Sir W. Pennington — Ramsdon, Loch Laggen	90,000 acres
The Earl of Ancaster	81,000 acres
The Duke of Roxburghe	80,000 acres

Who Owns Inverness-shire?

Here are the acreages of the 5 principal landowners from the official government 1872-73 survey:—

1.	Lord Lovat	161,574
2.	Earl of Seafield, Balmacaan, Glen Urquhart and Castle Grant, Grantown	160,224
3.	Evan Baillie of Dochfour, Kingussie	141,148
4.	Alexander A.E. Mackintosh, (The Mackintosh) Moy Hall	124,181
5.	Donald Cameron of Lochiel, Achnacarry Castle	109,874

The successors of 4 out of 5 of the above lairds still retain much the same enormous acreages to this day. The only one of the quintet whose holdings have been drastically reduced is the Mackintosh of Mackintosh, but though four fifths of his estate may be dispersed, most people would look upon 24,000 acres as enough.

One apparent change is purely nominal. Dochfour is owned by Lord Burton; but his grandfather Baillie married Nellie Lisa Bass, obviously no small beer with such a surname, who succeeded, by special remainder, her father the first Lord Burton as a baroness in her own right to be followed in line by her grandson, the present peer. A further 24,500 acres in Ross-shire diversifies the Baillie/Burton holdings.

Sixty years ago, the report of the Scottish Land Enquiry Committee put "The Relation of Sporting Interests to Rural Industry" in a nutshell: "The most outstanding form of this exercise of the monopoly power in the matter of the indulgence of personal pleasure as opposed to the national economic interests of a rural population occurs in the case of game preservation". This was set down by an independent body appointed by the Chancellor of the Exchequer to obtain an accurate and impartial account of social and economic conditions in rural areas.

There are 52 deer forests in Inverness-shire representing, at a conservative estimate at least 802,449 acres. This is out of a Scottish total of 2,798,706 acres, but it is never easy to present precise statistics of deer ground, as it may be incorporated with hill-farming and other usages. A more recent (1969) Highland

Development Board spokesman figured "Three and a half million acres exclusively preserved for deer, of the seven million acres over which deer roam to a greater or lesser extent." As venison marketed from Scotland's 185-190,000 deer amounts to some 1,500 tons, valued in the region of £450,000 (calculated in terms of output as equivalent to what could be produced from 6,000 acres of arable land), little wonder that the Board's speaker questioned whether the enormous deer forest acreage was "being utilised in the best interests of the national economy".

It has been worked out that the average gross yield from deer is three-quarters of a pound of venison per acre, just as the same area of grouse moor produced one and a half pounds of grouse, and half a mountain hare; so when next you put down a lid on your delicately simmering joint of venison (which you are more likely to do if you live in West Germany than here), you know now that a good-sized slice of the Scottish Highlands has gone to pot for another year.

From a pamphlet called 'Acre-ocracy' compiled by John McEwan for the Perthshire Fabian Society.

Tour Schedule

Tour 1 : 1973

24	April	Aberdeen Arts Centre
25/26		MacRobert Centre, Stirling
27		Little Theatre, Inverness
28		Fortrose Town Hall
1	May	Kinlochbervie Town Hall
2		Lochinver Town Hall
3		Achiltibuie Town Hall
4		Ullapool, The Caledonian Hotel
5		Dornie Town Hall
8		Broadford Town Hall, Skye
9		Portree Town Hall, Skye
10		Tarbert Hall, Harris
11		Stornoway, The Caberfeidh Hotel
15		Brora Community Centre
16		Pittentrail Hall, Rogart
17		Averon Community Centre, Alness
18		Dingwall Town Hall
19		Portgower Hall
21		Stromness Community Centre, Orkney
22		Cosmo Ballroom, Kirkwall, Orkney
23		Orphir Community Centre
24		Town Hall, Thurso
25		The Hall, Bonar Bridge
26		Corrin Halls, Oban
30		Harbour Arts Centre, Irvine
31		Livingston
1/2	June	Cottage Theatre, Cumbernauld

Tour 2 : 1973

18	September	Aberdeen Arts Centre
19		Torry Academy Hall, Aberdeen
20		Dalrymple Hall, Fraserburgh
21		Tain Town Hall
22		Shinness Hall

24		Dingwall Academy
25		Scourie Hall
26		Ullapool Hall
27		Ness Hall
28		Nicholson Institute, Stornoway
29		Leverburgh Hall, Harris
2	October	Lochmaddy Hall
3		Benbecula Community Hall
4		Kyleakin Hall
5		Lochcarron Hall
6		Poolewe Hall
11/12		Palais des Beaux Arts, Brussels
13		Proka Zaal Ghent
16		Skerray Hall, Rogart
17		Arday Hall, Strathy
18		Golspie Assembly Hall
19		Durness Hall
20		Wick Assembly Rooms
25		Portnaven Hall, Portaskaig, Islay
26		Bowmore Hall, Portnahaven
30	October/	
	10 November	Citizens' Theatre, Glasgow
19	November/	
	1 December	Royal Lyceum Theatre, Edinburgh

Tour 3 : 1974

18/22 June		Abbey Theatre, Dublin
24		Gurranabraher Community Hall, Cork
25		Drumgeelly Community Centre, Shannon
27		Leisureland H...
28		Westport To...
29		Sligo Town ...